W9-AGS-732

The Everyday Song Book

By
Connie Walters

Inside Page Illustrations By
Diane Totten

Cover Illustration By
Ann Lutnicki

Publishers
T.S. Denison & Company, Inc.
Minneapolis, Minnesota 55431

Dedication

To my loving husband, Herman, who has given me so much support and encouragement, enabling me to grow and develop, and in turn, give to others.

Connie Walters, Author

Acknowledgments

My sincere gratitude to these special people who were very helpful during the preparation of this book:

To Diane Totten for her ongoing support of my work and her animated illustrations which bring life to my lyrics;

To Molly Brown and Marianne Pniewski who were always willing to test out my new songs;

To teachers Carol Salesky and Chris Rea for their input;

To my friends, Ron and Vicky Loyd, Jeanette McCrickard, and Gail Ketola who took time to listen and give feedback;

To Carol Thiry for her dedicated work in editing;

To librarian, Pat Waters, for her research on copyright;

To my nephews Jim and Scott O'Leary who inspired and motivated me;

To my granddaughter, Jasmine, whose enthusiasm sparked my creativity.

And to my children: Dawn, Debbie, Stephen, Cheryl-Lynn, and Kevin who showed their support in so many ways.

T.S. DENISON & COMPANY, INC.

Standard Book Number 513–02176–0
The Everyday Song Book
Copyright © 1993 by T.S. Denison & Co., Inc.
9601 Newton Avenue South
Minneapolis, Minnesota 55431

Introduction

Singing in the classroom should not be reserved just for music time—songs can be sung at various times throughout the day. Singing songs is an excellent way to teach a lesson, give directions, or capture a child's attention. Children respond with added attentiveness when a teacher's questions, requests, and directives are sung to enjoyable melodies. *The Everyday Song Book* is a book filled with lyrics written to fun and familiar melodies. It also includes a few all-time favorites such as "Down By The Bay," "Aiken Drum," "Five Little Ducks," and "Alice The Camel."(Music for all melodies is provided in the back of the book.)

The first section of this book provides the teacher with lyrics to meet every need throughout the class session. There are songs for energetic times as well as for quiet times; songs for cleaning up, going outside, and going for walks; songs for fire safety, good manners, sneezes, and colds; and most importantly, songs for enhancing self-esteem.

In the second section of *The Everyday Song Book*, the teacher will find songs to teach very basic essentials such as counting, adding, subtracting, colors, and shapes. Also included in this section are activities to reinforce this learning. Patterns are provided as a visual means for teaching the lyrics. Research shows that using more than one sense reinforces learning; therefore, the teacher is encouraged to use the auditory and visual senses.

Suggestions for using the patterns are:
- Color brightly; children enjoy vivid colors.
- Protect the pieces with laminating film or contact paper; they will last longer.
- Attach pellon, sandpaper, or felt tape on the back of each piece for use on the flannel board.
- Attach magnetic tape on the back of each piece for use on the magnetic board.
- Store in a large envelope, plastic bag, or manila folder; include the song with the pieces.

The teacher is encouraged to be creative with the class by changing lyrics, adding verses, and writing songs as opportunities and needs arise. When singing the lyrics, be aware that the number of syllables in a line do not always fit the exact number of notes in a melody and you may need to add or subtract notes to accommodate new words. It is also important to remember that young children respond to a teacher's enjoyment and enthusiasm in singing rather than the quality or excellence of the teacher's singing voice. Making up songs throughout the day will model for the children how simple and pleasurable singing can be. Be flexible and have fun!

Table of Contents

Section Two
Songs for Basic Learning

Songs Throughout The Day

Greetings
Name Songs
Self-Esteem
Clean Up Time
Transition Songs
Snack Time
Action Songs
Quiet Time
Good Manners
Health
Safety
Good-Bye

GREETING SONGS

Greeting songs are often sung when children are called together for circle time and music time. Greetings can also be sung at various times throughout the day: during dramatic play, at story time, at snack time, as children arrive at school, and whenever the teacher likes. Verses can be shortened and words can be changed to fit the situation.

GOOD MORNING
(Melody: A Tisket, A Tasket)

Good morning, good morning
It's time to say "good morning"
Another day has just begun
I know that we'll have lots of fun!

Good morning, good morning
It's time to say "good morning"
I'm very glad that you could come
So we can play and have some fun!

GOOD AFTERNOON
(Melody: The Mulberry Bush)

It's time to say "Good afternoon"
Good afternoon, good afternoon
It's time to say "good afternoon"
What fun we'll have today!

We're going to play with all the toys*
All the toys, all the toys
We're going to play with all the toys
What fun we'll have today!

* Sing additional verses naming other activities scheduled for that day's program such as "We're going to paint some pictures."

HELLO TIME
(Melody: Oh, Susanna)

Oh, it's time to say hello, hello
Hello and how are you?
Oh, it's time to say hello, hello
To everyone of you.

Hello friends,* a big "hello" to you!
We will sing and play and laugh today
Yes, this is what we'll do.

* Substitute with "boys," "girls," "children,"
"teacher," "parents," or individual names.

HELLO SONG
(Melody: Polly Wolly Doodle)

Oh, I'd like to say hello, hello
Hello—how do you do?
Oh, I'd like to say hello, hello
To you, and you, and you.

How are you? How are you?
How are you, my little friend?
I'm so very glad to see you
Yes, so very glad to see you!
Oh, I know that we'll have fun today!

HI THERE!
(Melody: Shoo, Fly)

Hi there, so glad you came
Hi there, so glad you came
Hi there, so glad you came
1-2-3 let's shout "hurray!"
Hurray! *(spoken)*

Hi there, so glad you're here
Hi there, so glad you're here
Hi there, so glad you're here
1-2-3 let's give a cheer!
Yea! *(spoken)*

*Teacher can shake hands with
the children as this song is sung.*

Sing the first verse using a puppet hidden inside a box. For the second verse, invite the children to imitate the actions of the puppet. They should squat low on the floor and pretend to be hiding in a box. At the sound of the clap, all should pop up.

SURPRISE
(Melody: I'm A Little Teapot)

Where is Sammy hiding, do you see?
Inside a box as quiet as can be
Press the magic button and you'll see
He will pop up 1-2-3! (clap)
(Sammy the Snake puppet pops up and shouts: "Surprise!")

Where are all the children can you see?*
Inside a box as quiet as can be
Press the magic button and you'll see
They will pop up 1-2-3! (clap)
(Children pop up and shout "Surprise!")

* Variations:
  Where are all the boys now, do you see?
  Where are all the girls now, do you see?

Directions for Sammy the Snake puppet

1. Make a simple sock puppet for your "Sammy the Snake" using a colorful knee-high sock.
2. Trim him with buttons, felt, fake fur, yarn, rickrack, sequins, etc.
3. Cut a hole in the top and bottom of a box large enough for your hand to fit through.
4. Insert Sammy through the bottom opening and have him pop up through the top opening.

For many children, a school setting often offers the first opportunity to establish friendships and interact with others on a regular basis.

I WANT TO BE YOUR FRIEND
(Melody: Jimmy Crack Corn)

Look at me and smile hello
Look at me and smile hello
Look at me and smile hello
I want to be your friend.

Look at me and wave hello
Look at me and wave hello
Look at me and wave hello
I want to be your friend.

Look at me and wink your eye
Look at me and wink your eye
Look at me and wink your eye
I want to be your friend.

Look at me and shake my hand
Look at me and shake my hand
Look at me and shake my hand
I want to be your friend.

FRIENDS
(Melody: You Are My Sunshine)

You are my friend: I'm your friend too!
I like to play and run with you
I like to jump with you
I like to skip with you.

You are my friend; I'm your friend too!
I like to sit and read with you
I like to paint with you
I like to color with you
Let's have fun together today!

Getting to know more about one another strengthens friendships. Suggest that the children invite parents or grandparents to class to share their ethnic origins. Ask the visitors to bring an item which represents their ancestors' native land and perhaps an ethnic food for the children to taste.

GREETINGS (In Various Languages)
(Melody: Bluebird)

Hello, hello everybody
Hello, hello everybody
Hello, hello everybody
So very glad to see you.

Hola, hola, everybody
Hola, hola, everybody
Hola, hola, everybody
So very glad to see you.

Shalom, Shalom everybody
Shalom, Shalom everybody
Shalom, Shalom everybody
So very glad to see you.

Bonjour, bonjour, everybody
Bonjour, bonjour, everybody
Bonjour, bonjour, everybody
So very glad to see you.

Buenos dias, everybody
Buenos dias, everybody
Buenos dias, everybody
So very glad to see you.

Show pictures of children from various countries as you sing a greeting in the spoken language of that country.

Spanish: Buenos Dias, Hola
French: Bonjour
German: Guten Tag
Italian: Buon Giorno
Swahili: Jambo
Norwegian: God *(goo)* Dag

Hawaiian: Aloha
Hebrew: Shalom
Japanese: Konichiwa
Chinese: Ni Hao Ma
Russian: Dobroze Utro
Polish: Dzien Dobry

NAME SONGS

The following melodies will allow the teacher to sing each child's name even if the class size is large. Repeat the song of your choice until the children's names have been sung.

CHILDREN'S NAMES
(Melody: Ten Little Indians)
Joshua, Christopher, Kathy, and Eric
Elizabeth, Marianne, Patrick, and Molly
Jonathan, Anthony, Becky, and Susan
They are sitting down!

ALL MY FRIENDS
(Melody: The Farmer In The Dell)
Oh, Dawn is my friend
And Debbie is my friend
Stephen, Kevin, Cheryl-Lynn
They all are my friends.

MY FRIENDS AT SCHOOL
(Melody: For He's A Jolly Good Fellow)
The teacher sat down in the circle
The teacher sat down in the circle
The teacher sat down in the circle
To see who came to school

Now, tell me who is here
Now, tell me who is here

There's Becky, Jimmy, and Julie
There's Charity, Richie, and Danny
There's Justin, Kelly, and Michael
These are my good friends at school.

Now tell me, are there more?
Now tell me, are there more?...

HERE WE ARE TOGETHER
(Melody: Did You Ever See A Lassie?)
Here we are together, together, together
Here we are together and happy are we!
There's Timothy and Kyra and Chantal and Brian*
Here we are together and happy are we!

* *Continue singing all of the children's names here.*

Although most children do not object to their names being sung in a group song, some children are very uncomfortable when singled out. Ask each child's permission to sing a song about him or her. Respect the child's decision.

WHERE ARE YOU?
(Melody: Paw Paw Patch)

Where, oh where, oh where is Erica?
Where, oh where, oh where is Erica?
Where, oh where, oh where is Erica?
She is sitting nicely on the floor.

Where, oh where, oh where is Nicholas?
Where, oh where, oh where is Nicholas?
Where, oh where, oh where is Nicholas?
He is sitting quietly on the floor.

COME AND PLAY
(Melody: Are You Sleeping?)

Where is Jasmine? Where is Jasmine?
There she is, there she is.
How are you today? How are you today?
Come and play, come and play.

Where is Chandler? Where is Chandler?
Stand up tall, stand up tall.*
How are you today? How are you today?
Come and play, come and play.

* *Variations:*
   Wave your hand, smile at me,
   Tap your head, tap your shoulder…

Name Game:
The teacher sits facing the children and invites the class to sing the song "Come And Play" to one child. At the end of the song, the child named comes over to sit with the teacher. The process is then repeated until all the children are seated with the teacher. For a large group of children, shorten the process by singing the first two lines of the song to 3–4 children at a time. Then add the last two lines.

Ask each child if you may sing about him or her. Give the child a choice as to which animal (cat, dog, or horse) will play the fiddle for his/her verse. Of course, they may choose to name a different animal.

SING A NAME
(Melody: refrain from
Boom, Boom, Ain't It Great To Be Crazy?)

Let's sing a song about Jennie
Let's sing a song about Jennie
Cat with the fiddle
And three white mice
Let's sing a song about Jennie.

Oh, Jennie Johnson has brown hair
Oh, Jennie Johnson has brown eyes
Cat with the fiddle
And three white mice
How nice to sing about Jennie!

Let's sing a song about Billy
Let's sing a song about Billy
Dog with the fiddle
And three white mice
Let's sing a song about Billy.

Oh, Billy Adams has blond hair
Oh, Billy Adams has blue eyes
Dog with the fiddle
And three white mice
How nice to sing about Billy!

Let's sing a song about Megan
Let's sing a song about Megan
Horse with the fiddle
And three white mice
Let's sing a song about Megan.

Megan O'Leary has red hair
Megan O'Leary has green eyes
Horse with the fiddle
And three white mice
How nice to sing about Megan!

SELF-ESTEEM

Enhancing the development of a child's self-esteem should be a very important goal for educators. Encourage each child to develop his or her unique gifts and talents. Help each child to feel that he or she is lovable and has something worthwhile to offer the world. The following songs will reinforce this development.

JUST ONE ME
(Melody: Twinkle, Twinkle)

Look around and you will see
There is no one just like me!
No one has a face like mine
No one has my hair or eyes
I am special—yes indeed
I know there is just one me!

I AM SO VERY SPECIAL
(Melody: Pretty Little Dutch Girl)

I am so very special
As special as can be
Just look around and you will see
There's no one just like me!

I'M UNIQUE
(Melody: Jimmy Crack Corn)

Oh, you can look all over town
And search the world up and down
You will never-never see
Someone who's just like me!

I'M GLAD I AM ME
(Melody: B-I-N-G-O)

Oh, look around and you will see
There is no one just like me
I'm glad I am me!
I'm glad I am me!
I'm glad I am me!
There is no one just like me.

The illustrations on the following pages will add to the enjoyment of this song. Copy, color, cut out, laminate, and secure felt or magnetic tape on the back of each picture to use on a felt or magnetic board.

GLAD TO BE ME
(Melody: My Bonnie Lies Over The Ocean)

Now, ostrich was telling her baby   *(put up ostriches)*
I want you to hold your head high
If ever your friends start to tease you
Just say to them as you walk by—

I am special
I know there's no one like me—like me
I am special
I'm so very glad to be me!

The hippo was telling his baby   *(put up hippos)*
It's true that you're big as can be
But you'll always be very special
I want you to say it with me—

I am special
I know there's no one like me—like me
I am special
I'm so very glad to be me!

Orangutan said to her baby   *(put up orangutans)*
With very long arms you can swing
But others may look at you strangely
So this is what you have to sing—

I am special
I know there's no one like me—like me
I am special
I'm so very glad to be me!

Now, daddy giraffe told his baby   *(put up giraffes)*
It's true that you'll never be small
Just tell all the world that you're special
And hold your head up very tall!

I am special
I know there's no one like me—like me
I am special
I'm so very glad to be me!

GLAD TO BE ME

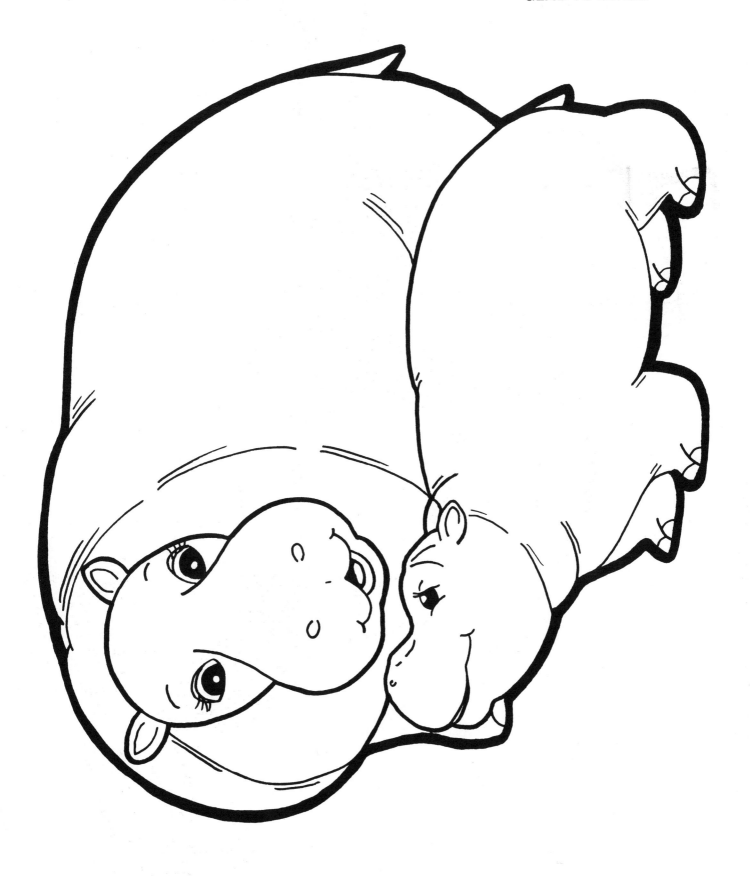

GLAD TO BE ME

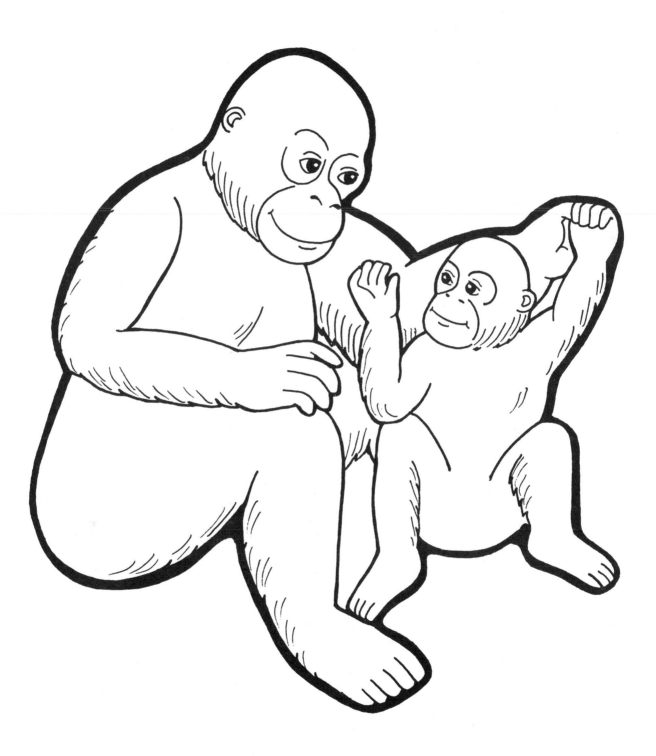

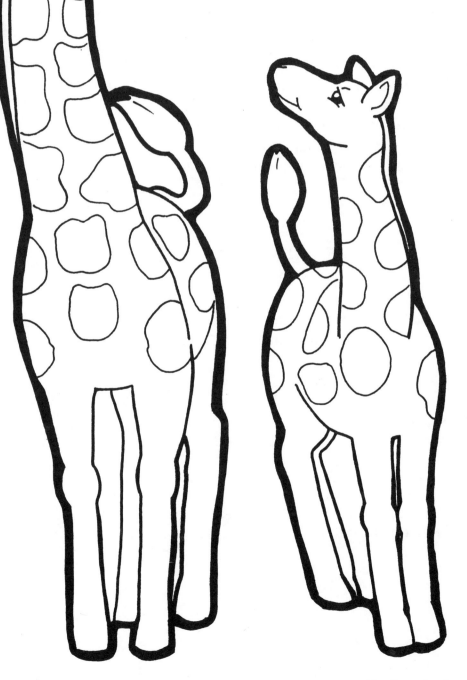

CLEAN UP TIME

Use your favorite melody to write your own clean up song. You are an excellent model for the children. From watching you, they will learn to put their own words to melodies and sing about any activity which they are undertaking.

WE'RE PICKING UP THE TOYS
(Melody: The Farmer In The Dell)

We're picking up the toys
We're picking up the toys
We'll put them away for another day
We're picking up the toys.

THIS IS THE WAY WE CLEAN UP THE ROOM
(Melody: The Mulberry Bush)

This is the way we clean up the room
Clean up the room, clean up the room
This is the way we clean up the room
We put the toys away.

PICK UP THE BLOCKS
(Melody: Paw Paw Patch)

Pick up the blocks and put them away
Pick up the blocks and put them away
Pick up the blocks and put them away
Put them away for some other day.

CLEAN UP TIME
(Melody: This Old Man)

Clean up time, clean up time
Everything will look just fine
We will pick up the toys and put them all away
We can play another day.

Children love when you mention their name in the clean up songs. Soon you will hear them shouting: "I'm putting the crayons away. Sing about me!"

ARE YOU CLEANING?
(Melody: Are You Sleeping?)

Are you cleaning? Are you cleaning?
Cleaning up? Cleaning up?
Janelle is putting the blocks away
Scott is putting the trucks away
We're cleaning up the room
We're cleaning up the room.

Photocopy, color, and cut out the illustration of Esmerelda, the octopus who likes to clean up. Display the picture at the children's eye level. Discuss with them the importance of sharing responsibility for taking good care of things at school.

ESMERELDA
(Melody: Alouette)

Esmerelda tells us that it's time now
Time to stop and put away the toys.

Time to put away the blocks?
Time to put away the blocks!
And the trucks? And the trucks!
And the dolls? And the dolls!

Esmerelda tells us that it's time now
Time to stop and put away the toys.

Time to put away the paint?
Time to put away the paint!
And the chalk? And the chalk!
And the glue? And the glue!

Esmerelda tells us that it's time now
Time to stop and put away the toys.

ESMERELDA

TRANSITION SONGS

Use simple and enjoyable melodies to sing your instructions to the children. They will sing along as they comply with your directives.

GETTING IN LINE
(Melody: Blue Bird)

Quiet, quiet, let's be quiet
Quiet, quiet, let's be quiet
Quiet, quiet, let's be quiet
We want it very quiet.

Stand up, stand up and be quiet
Stand up, stand up and be quiet
Stand up, stand up and be quiet
We're standing and we're quiet.

Slowly, slowly get in line now
Slowly, slowly get in line now
Slowly, slowly get in line now
We're getting in a line now.

Softly, softly, walk so softly
Softly, softly, walk so softly
Softly, softly, walk so softly
We're walking very softly.

Children can hum the melody as they continue to walk to their destination. When you have arrived, hum the verse for the last time. Add "Shhh!!" at the very end.

GOING DOWNSTAIRS
(Melody: Down By The Station)

Hand on the handrail
We'll go **down** together
Walking very carefully
All in a row
We'll walk very slowly
We're not in a hurry
Let's be quiet
As we go!

Hand on the handrail
We'll go **up** together
Walking very carefully
All in a row
We'll walk very slowly
We're not in a hurry
Let's be quiet
As we go!

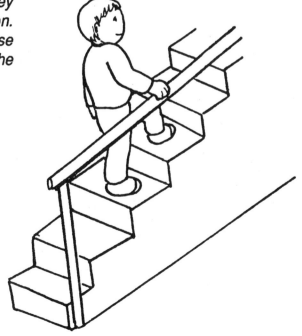

GOING OUTSIDE
(Melody: All The Fish)

Children, now it's time
    to put our boots on
Time to put our boots on
Time to put our boots on
Children, now it's time
    to put our boots on
We're going out!

Children, now it's time
    to put our coats on
Time to put our coats on
Time to put our coats on
Children, now it's time
    to put our coats on
We're going out!

Children, now it's time
    to put our hats on
Time to put our hats on
Time to put our hats on
Children, now it's time
    to put our hats on
We're going out!

For fun and variety, sing different familiar melodies with the lyrics below as you go for a long walk.

GOING FOR A WALK # 1
(Melody: London Bridge)

We are going for a walk
For a walk, for a walk
We are going for a walk
Oh, what fun!

GOING FOR A WALK # 2
(Melody: Looby-Loo)

We're going for a walk
It's very far away
We're going for a walk
Oh, what a wonderful day!

GOING FOR A WALK # 3
(Melody: The Farmer In The Dell)

What fun we'll have today
What fun we'll have today
We are going for a walk
What fun we'll have today!

SNACK TIME

Singing a song is an excellent attention-getter. As the children are engaged in conversation at the snack table, sing "Let's Be Quiet" from the Quiet Time section and they will join you. Direct them to place their hands on their lap with the song "Hands In Your Lap" and then invite them to join you in singing "Snack Time Thanks." Establish these three songs as a class routine for snack time.

HANDS IN YOUR LAP
(Melody: London Bridge)

Put your hands right in your lap
In your lap, in your lap
Put your hands right in your lap
We'll have a snack.

APPLE CRUNCH
(Melody: Three Blind Mice)

Apple crunch, apple crunch
Crunch, crunch, crunch
Crunch, crunch, crunch
We're making apple crunch today!
What fun it is to crunch away!
Crunch, crunch, crunch
Crunch, crunch, crunch.

SNACK TIME THANKS
(Melody: Are You Sleeping?)

Let's be thankful *(echo)*
Let's be glad *(echo)*
For the many good things *(echo)*
That we have *(echo)*.

Divide the children into two groups and sing the song responsively.

Invite each child to make an individual portion of apple crunch.
Sing "Apple Crunch" with the children as they crumble their crackers.

Recipe for Easy Apple Crunch
Ingredients (individual serving):
   5 graham cracker squares and applesauce.

1. Child crumbles one graham cracker square onto waxed paper and pours the crumbs into small bowl.
2. Teacher spoons applesauce on top of cracker crumbs.
3. Child repeats step 1.
4. Teacher spoons more applesauce over crackers.
5. Child crumbles one graham cracker on top.
6. Serve cold or slightly heated in microwave.

For a smaller serving size, give each child three squares of crackers and omit steps 3 and 4.

ACTION SONGS

A few simple action songs are a valuable aid to the teacher for remedying the children's need to move around. These songs can be sung at circle time, before story time, between stories, or whenever they are needed.

FROM HEAD TO FOOT
(Melody: Mary Had A Little Lamb)

Turn your head from side to side
Side to side, side to side
Turn your head from side to side
From side to side and stop!

Lift your shoulders up and down
Up and down, up and down
Lift your shoulders up and down
Up and down and stop!

Shake, shake, shake your hands and arms
Hands and arms, hands and arms
Shake, shake, shake your hands and arms
Shake, shake, shake, and stop!

Wiggle your hips from side to side
Side to side, side to side
Wiggle your hips from side to side
Side to side and stop!

Slide your foot—go back and forth
Back and forth, back and forth
Slide your foot—go back and forth
Back and forth and stop!

Sit right down and rest awhile
Rest awhile, rest awhile
Sit right down and rest awhile
Rest awhile and smile!

TAP, STAND, AND JUMP
(Melody: This Old Man)

Tap your head, tap your nose
Tap your knees and touch your toes
Now stand up and stretch your arms
    right up to the sky
Jump real fast and jump real high!
STOP! *(shout)*

Tap your cheek, tap your chin
Tap your chest and touch your shin
Now stand up and stretch your arms
    right up to the sky
Jump real fast and jump real high.
STOP! *(shout)*

Tap your shoulders, tap your knees
Tap your ankles and touch your feet
Now stand up and stretch your arms
    right up to the sky
Jump real fast and jump real high.
STOP! *(shout)*

Sit right down on the ground
Quietly without a sound
Now take your hands and put them
    in your lap
Close your eyes and take a nap.

LISTEN AND DO
(Melody: Oh, A Hunting We Will Go)

Oh, my teacher says "Stand up"
And then she* says "Sit down"
Oh, I sit down; I stand up
And then I walk around.
STOP! *(shout)*

Oh, my teacher says "Bend low"
And then she* says "Jump high"
Oh, I jump high; I bend low
And then I walk around.
STOP! *(shout)*

Oh, my teacher says "Skate slow"
And then she* says "Hop fast"
Oh, I hop fast; I skate slow
And then I walk around.
STOP! *(shout)*

* Use "she" *or* "he" as appropriate.

THE BODY SHAKE
(Melody: Dry Bones)
Instruct the children to lie on their back.

Now lift and shake your right hand †
Now lift and shake your left hand
Now lift and shake your two hands
Now rest them both on the ground.

Now lift and shake your right foot †
Now lift and shake your left foot
Now lift and shake your two feet
Now rest them both on the ground.

Now lift and shake your right elbow †
Now lift and shake your left elbow
Now lift and shake your two elbows
Now rest them both on the ground.

Now lift and shake your head
Now lift and shake your two arms
Now lift and shake your two legs
Now rest them both on the ground.

† For very young children omit "right" and "left" and sing:
   Now lift and shake just one hand (foot, elbow)
   Now lift and shake the other hand (foot, elbow)

QUIET TIME

Many times the children need to be quieted down, such as at the end of a busy day, following a very energetic activity, or when the class is too loud or too noisy. When sung softly, the melodies in this section should produce a calming effect.

LET'S BE QUIET
(Melody: Are You Sleeping?)

Let's be quiet, let's be quiet
Don't say a word, don't say a word
We want it very quiet
We want it very quiet
Don't say a word, don't say a word.

BE STILL
(Melody: Hush, Little Baby)

Feet be quiet—don't make a sound
Be real still—don't move around.

Legs be quiet—don't make a sound
Be real still—don't move around.

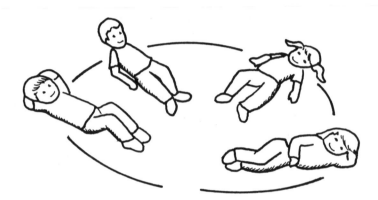

Hands be quiet—don't make a sound
Be real still—don't move around.

Arms be quiet—don't make a sound
Be real still—don't move around.

Head be quiet—don't make a sound
Be real still—don't move around.

Shhhhhh!

REST TIME
(Melody: Michael, Row The Boat Ashore)

Now, it's time for us to rest—let's be quiet
Now, it's time for us to rest—let's be quiet.

We've been busy all day long—let's be quiet
We've been busy all day long—let's be quiet.

Close your eyes for just awhile—let's be quiet
Close your eyes for just awhile—let's be quiet.

DREAMS
(Melody: Sailing, Sailing)

Let's be quiet; it's time to go to sleep*
Just close your eyes for just awhile
And count the pretty sheep.

Dream of sunshine and the ocean blue
Oh, see all the waves go in and out
And splash all over you.

* *Variation:* Let's be quiet; now don't let out a peep

HUSH-A-BYE
(Melody: Kum Ba Ya)

Go to sleep now, hush-a-bye
Sandman's coming by and by
Dream of moon and stars so high
Dear little child, hush-a-bye.

GOOD MANNERS

The old adage "good manners are caught and not taught" is true. However, discussing and singing about good manners reinforces awareness and appreciation of this social behavior.

SAY IT POLITELY
(Melody: If You're Happy And You Know It)

When I ask my dad for something, I say "please"
When I ask my mom for something, I say "please"
I can see it makes them happy
When I say it so politely
Yes, good manners means to always ask them "please."

When my grandpa gives me something, I say "thank you"
When my grandma gives me something, I say "thank you"
I can see it makes them happy
When I say it so politely
Yes, good manners means to always say "thank you."

If I bump into someone I say "excuse me"
If I need to interrupt, I say "excuse me"
I can see it makes people happy
When I say it so politely
Yes, good manners means to always say "excuse me."

If I spill my drink at lunch I say "I'm sorry"
If I break something of yours I say "I'm sorry"
I can see it makes you happy
When I say it so politely
Yes, good manners means to always say "I'm sorry."

MAGIC WORDS
(Melody: Going To Kentucky)

I say that I am sorry
Excuse me, if you please
Oh, thank you and you're welcome
I must remember these!
(repeat)

HEALTH

Pass out tissues to each of the children to use as they sing the sneeze songs. Invite them to use the tissues when they sing "ah choo." Demonstrate how to catch a sneeze in the crook of their elbow if they are unable to get a tissue in time.

SNEEZE SONG
(Melody: The Farmer In The Dell)

My nose is tickling me
I think I'm going to sneeze
I need a tissue now;
Excuse me, if you please—AH CHOO!

CATCH THAT SNEEZE
(Melody: Chiapenecas)

I think that I'm going to sneeze—ah choo!
I think that I'm going to sneeze—ah choo!
'Scuse me—I need a tissue
'Scuse me—I need a tissue
'Scuse me—I'll get one
Now I'm ready to catch my next sneeze—AH CHOO!

Act out the following two songs with a puppet singing the words. Have the puppet talk to the children about staying in bed when they are sick and resting until they have fully recovered.

I HAVE A COLD
(Melody: I Had A Rooster)

I have a bad cold, boo-hoo, boo-hoo!
My mom says I must stay in bed, boo-hoo!
I'd rather go out and play today
Play baseball, go swimming, blow bubbles, Hooray!

STAYING IN BED
(Melody: You Are My Sunshine)

I want to get dressed and go outside now
Because it's such a sunny day
But I don't feel well; I ache all over!
Covered up, in my bed I'll stay!

SAFETY

A catchy tune entices children to repeat a song over and over again. This is an excellent way to teach the important lessons of pedestrian, traffic, and fire safety.

BEFORE I CROSS THE STREET
(Melody: It Ain't Gonna Rain)

I look to the left; I look to the right
I look to the left again
I will always look both ways
Before I cross the street.

I look to the left; I look to the right
I look to the left again
I will always look and listen
Before I use my feet.

THE TRAFFIC LIGHT
(Melody: The People On The Bus)

What do you do when the light turns red?
The light turns red, the light turns red?
What do you do when the light turns red?
Red means you stop.

What do you do when the light turns yellow?
The light turns yellow, the light turns yellow?
What do you do when the light turns yellow?
Yellow means you wait.

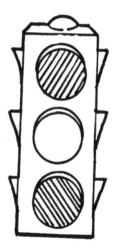

What do you do when the light turns green?
The light turns green, the light turns green?
What do you do when the light turns green?
Green means you go.

BUCKLE UP
(Melody: Aiken Drum)

My daddy drives me to the school
To the school, to the school
My daddy drives me to the school
And this is what we do!

We buckle up our seat belts
Our seat belts, our seat belts
We buckle up our seat belts
Yes, this is what we do!

My mommy drives me to the store
To the store, to the store
My mommy drives me to the store
Yes, this is what we do!

We buckle up our seat belts
Our seat belts, our seat belts
We buckle up our seat belts
Yes, this is what we do!

My grandpa drives me to the zoo
To the zoo, to the zoo
My grandpa drives me to the zoo
And this is what we do!

We buckle up our seat belts
Our seat belts, our seat belts
We buckle up our seat belts
Yes, this is what we do!

My grandma drives me to the show
To the show, to the show
My grandma drives me to the show
And this is what we do!

We buckle up our seat belts
Our seat belts, our seat belts
We buckle up our seat belts
Yes, this is what we do!

The consequence of fire damage can be very serious. Therefore, teachers must review classroom procedures and fire-safety actions regularly. The following songs will enable a child to commit these safety actions to memory.

FIRE SAFETY
(Melody: Skip To My Lou)

I found matches what do I do?
I found matches what do I do?
I found matches what do I do?
I'll throw them away or give them to you.

I see a fire, what do I do?
I see a fire, what do I do?
I see a fire, what do I do?
I'll get help—that's what I'll do!

If my clothes catch on fire
If my clothes catch on fire
If my clothes catch on fire
I will know just what to do:

Stop, drop; lay down and roll
Stop, drop; lay down and roll
Stop, drop; lay down and roll
This is what we all should do.

STOP, DROP, LAY DOWN, AND ROLL
(Melody: B-I-N-G-O)

If your clothes should catch on fire
This is what to do—
Stop, drop, lay down and roll
Stop, drop, lay down and roll
Stop, drop, lay down and roll
'Cause this puts out the fire.

GOOD-BYE
At the end of class time, talk to the children about the enjoyable experiences they had. Departing from school on a positive, happy note will leave them with good feelings about their experience. Singing a good-bye song will give them a melody to hum on their way home.

ADIOS
(Melody: refrain from Do Lord)

Let's say good-bye now
It's time for us to go
Let's say good-bye now
It's time for us to go
Let's say good-bye now
It's time for us to go
See you soon, Adios, Good-bye!

It's time to go now
What fun we had at school
It's time to go now
What fun we had at school
It's time to go now
What fun we had at school
See you soon, Adios, Good-bye!

GOOD-BYE TIME
(Melody: Mary Had A Little Lamb)

Now it's time to say good-bye
Say good-bye, say good-bye
Now it's time to say good-bye
We had fun at school!

TIME TO GO
(Melody: Jimmy Crack Corn)

Good-bye friends, it's time to go!
Good-bye friends, it's time to go!
Good-bye friends, it's time to go!
What fun I had with you.

Wave good-bye, it's time to go!
Wave again, it's time to go!
Wave once more, it's time to go!
I'll see you soon, my friend.

Songs for Basic Learning

Colors
Numbers/Counting
Numbers/Adding
Numbers/Subtracting
Shapes
Body Parts
Senses
Food Songs
Language

THE RAINBOW TRAIN
(Melody: The Mulberry Bush)

The rainbow train is coming to town
Coming to town, coming to town
The rainbow train is coming to town
It's moving very fast.

The rainbow train is full of toys
Full of toys, full of toys
The rainbow train is full of toys
For all the girls and boys.

The red car's filled with bats and balls
Bats and balls, bats and balls
The red car's filled with bats and balls
For all the girls and boys.

The orange car's filled with puzzles and blocks
Puzzles and blocks, puzzles and blocks
The orange car's filled with puzzles and blocks
For all the girls and boys.

The yellow car's filled with dolls and planes
Dolls and planes, dolls and planes
The yellow car's filled with dolls and planes
For all the girls and boys.

The green car's filled with cars and boats
Cars and boats, cars and boats
The green car's filled with cars and boats
For all the girls and boys.

The blue car's filled with whistles and drums
Whistles and drums, whistles and drums
The blue car's filled with whistles and drums
For all the girls and boys.

The purple car's filled with marbles and tops
Marbles and tops, marbles and tops
The purple car's filled with marbles and tops
For all the girls and boys.

Red and orange, yellow and green
Blue and purple cars I see
The rainbow train is here at last
I'm glad it came so fast!

THE CLOWN WITH THE BALLOONS
(Melody: Alouette)

(put up clown with five balloons)

Oh! See the clown with all the pretty colors
See the clown with all the big balloons
Do you want the red balloon?   *(point to red balloon)*
Yes, I want the red balloon
Red balloon. Red balloon.   *(move red balloon off to the side)*

Oh! See the clown with all the pretty colors
See the clown with all the big balloons
Do you want the green balloon?   *(point to green balloon)*
Yes, I want the green balloon
Green balloon. Green balloon.   *(move green balloon next to the red)*
Red balloon. Red balloon.

Oh! See the clown with all the pretty colors
See the clown with all the big balloons
Do you want the yellow balloon?   *(point to the yellow balloon)*
Yes, I want the yellow balloon
Yellow balloon. Yellow balloon.   *(move yellow balloon next to the green)*
Green balloon. Green balloon.
Red balloon. Red balloon.

Oh! See the clown with all the pretty colors
See the clown with all the big balloons
Do you want the blue balloon?   *(point to blue balloon)*
Yes, I want the blue balloon
Blue balloon. Blue balloon.   *(move blue balloon next to the yellow)*
Yellow balloon. Yellow balloon.
Green balloon. Green balloon.
Red balloon. Red balloon.

Oh! See the clown with all the pretty colors
See the clown with all the big balloons
Do you want the orange balloon?   *(point to orange balloon)*
Yes, I want the orange balloon
Orange balloon. Orange balloon.   *(move orange balloon next to the blue)*
Blue balloon. Blue balloon.
Yellow balloon. Yellow balloon.
Green balloon. Green balloon.
Red balloon. Red balloon.

Oh! Look at me with all the pretty colors!   *(point to self)*
Look at me with all the big balloons!   *(point to balloons off to the side)*

THE BUTTERFLY'S COLORS
(Melody: Billy Boy)

Oh where do you go, butterfly, butterfly
Oh, where do you go by and by?
Do you go so far away?
Do you ever stop to play?
Oh, please stop now so I can see your colors.

Oh where do you go, butterfly, butterfly
Oh, where do you go by and by?
Can you stay for just an hour?
You can come and see my flowers
Oh, please stop now so I can see your colors.

Oh where do you go, butterfly, butterfly
Oh, where do you go by and by?
Do you visit different lands?
Do you see things that are grand?
Oh, please stop now so I can see your colors.

MIXING COLORS
(Melody: Mary Wore A Red Dress)

Red and yellow make orange
Orange, orange—
Red and yellow make orange
How about that!

Yellow and blue make green
Green, green—
Yellow and blue make green
How about that!

Blue and red make purple
Purple, purple—
Blue and red make purple
How about that!

Red and white make pink
Pink, pink—
Red and white make pink
How about that!

White and black make gray
Gray, gray—
White and black make gray
How about that!

CATCH A FISH
(Melody: The Muffin Man)

Molly's going to catch a fish
Catch a fish, catch a fish
Molly's going to catch a fish
What color will it be?

Molly caught a purple fish
Purple fish, purple fish
Molly caught a purple fish
Now she's set him free!

Brendan's going to catch a fish
Catch a fish, catch a fish
Brendan's going to catch a fish
What color will it be?

Brendan caught a yellow fish
Yellow fish, yellow fish
Brendan caught a yellow fish
Now he's set him free!

Activities—Colors

Directed Art Activity: Each child will make a wall mural of a rainbow train to take home. (This may take three or four sessions to complete.) Provide each child with (a) one engine to color, photocopied from the illustration on page 44; or one black engine, traced from the outline of the illustration and cut from black construction paper (b) six boxcars, cut from six colors of construction paper (red, orange, yellow, green, blue, and purple) and (c) pictures cut from magazines or catalogs. On a long sheet of paper, each child will paste the engine followed by the boxcars in the correct color order of the rainbow. Instruct the children to begin on the left side of the paper. (As they sing the song, they will follow the pictures from the left to the right.) The children may elect to add train wheels. Two circles can be drawn or printed on with thread spools for each boxcar's set of wheels. Invite the children to select appealing "cargo" to paste on each boxcar.

Parent Involvement: On the day that the children take their "Rainbow Train" wall mural home, provide the parents with a copy of the song "The Rainbow Train" with a note suggesting that they sing the song with their child and substitute the particular items in their child's boxcars in place of the items in the original song.

Visual Aid: Use the illustration on page 45 for the song "The Clown With The Balloons." Color, cut, and laminate the clown. Cut out and laminate five large circles for balloons (red, orange, yellow, green, blue); tape yarn to each balloon. Secure felt or magnetic tape to the back of the clown and each balloon. Display the illustration on a felt or magnetic board so that it looks as if the clown is holding the balloons. As you sing, move one balloon at a time as the song page indicates.

Bulletin Board Display: Use the illustration "The Clown" on your bulletin board. Enlarge the picture of "The Clown" found on page 45. Cut out large colored circles for the balloons. Add yarn to each balloon. Display the illustration so that it looks as if the clown is holding the balloons.

Social: Direct the children to play a circle game. Make eight or more copies of the butterfly illustration found on page 46. Use three different colors for the wings of each butterfly. Laminate, cut out, and punch holes at the top. Tie enough yarn so that the children can wear the butterflies around their necks.

Directions:

1. Children hold hands and form a circle.
2. The teacher gives one child a butterfly to wear around his/her neck.
3. The child "flies" around inside the circle while the class sings the song "The Butterfly's Colors"; when the verse is over, the child stops in front of a child who then names the colors of the butterfly wings.
4. The teacher gives the second child a different colored butterfly and the game is repeated.

Art Project: Children will make butterflies for the song "The Butterfly's Colors." Trace the outline of the butterfly pattern. Cut butterfly shapes out of 8 1/2" x 11" manila paper. Fold the butterflies in half. Invite children to drip paint onto the opened butterfly. Fold and press with hands; unfold and let dry. The teacher secures one end of string onto the back of the butterfly with reinforced tape, and staples the other end of the string to a straw. Children can sing "The Butterfly's Colors" while swinging their butterfly from the straw.

Cognitive: Children play a game to reinforce color recognition. Cut and laminate colored construction paper in the shape of a fish. Put 2–3 paper clips on each fish. Provide children with fishing poles (dowel rods) with magnets attached to the ends. Sing "Catch A Fish" as children take turns naming the color of the fish they catch.

RAINBOW TRAIN

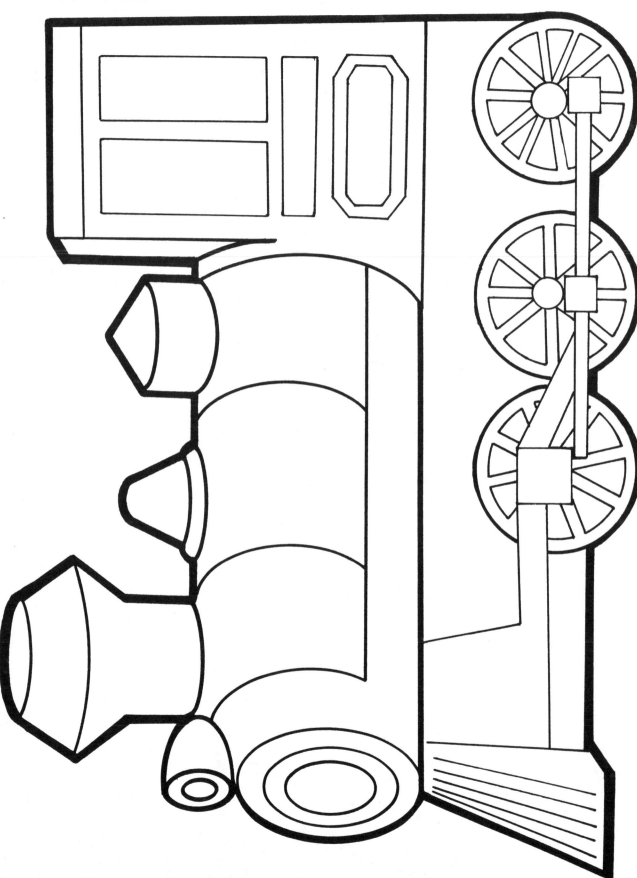

THE COUNTING SONG
(Melody: The Farmer In The Dell)

The puppy finds a bone	*(put up puppy)*
The puppy finds a bone	*(put up bone)*
I hear one little bark	
The puppy finds a bone—Ruff!	

The puppy finds two bones   *(put up second bone)*
The puppy finds two bones
I hear two little barks
The puppy finds two bones—Ruff, Ruff!

The puppy finds three bones   *(put up third bone)*
The puppy finds three bones
I hear three little barks
The puppy finds three bones—Ruff, Ruff, Ruff!

The hen lays an egg   *(put up hen)*
The hen lays an egg   *(put up egg)*
I hear one little cluck
The hen lays an egg—Cluck!

The hen lays two eggs   *(put up second egg)*
The hen lays two eggs
I hear two little clucks
The hen lays two eggs—Cluck, Cluck!

The hen lays three eggs   *(put up third egg)*
The hen lays three eggs
I hear three little clucks
The hen lays three eggs—Cluck, Cluck, Cluck!

The robin gets a worm   *(put up robin)*
The robin gets a worm   *(put up worm)*
I hear one little tweet
The robin gets a worm—Tweet!

The robin gets two worms   *(put up second worm)*
The robin gets two worms
I hear two little tweets
The robin gets two worms—Tweet, Tweet!

The robin gets three worms   *(put up third worm)*
The robin gets three worms
I hear three little tweets
The robin gets three worms—Tweet, Tweet, Tweet!

HOW MANY ANIMALS?
(Melody: Band of Angels)

There is one, there are two
There are three little panda bears
There are four, there are five
There are six little panda bears
There are seven, there are eight
There are nine little panda bears
Ten panda bears at the zoo.

Refrain:
Oh, let's go to the zoo
And see all the animals
See all the animals
See all the animals
Oh, let's go to the zoo
And see all the animals
The animals at the zoo.

There is one, there are two
There are three big gorillas
There are four, there are five
There are six big gorillas
There are seven, there are eight
There are nine big gorillas
Ten big gorillas at the zoo.
(refrain)

There is one, there are two
There are three fat elephants
There are four, there are five
There are six fat elephants
There are seven, there are eight
There are nine fat elephants
Ten fat elephants at the zoo.
(refrain)

There is one, there are two
There are three skinny monkeys
There are four, there are five
There are six skinny monkeys
There are seven, there are eight
There are nine skinny monkeys
Ten skinny monkeys at the zoo.
(refrain)

There is one, there are two
There are three tall giraffes
There are four, there are five
There are six tall giraffes
There are seven, there are eight
There are nine tall giraffes
Ten tall giraffes at the zoo.
(refrain)

There is one, there are two
There are three short penguins
There are four, there are five
There are six short penguins
There are seven, there are eight
There are nine short penguins
Ten short penguins at the zoo.
(refrain)

WALLABIES
(Melody: Ten Little Indians)

One little, two little
Three little wallabies
Four little, five little
Six little wallabies
Seven little, eight little
Nine little wallabies
Ten little wallabies
Jumping up and down.*

One little, two little
Three little wallabies
Four little, five little
Six little wallabies
Seven little, eight little
Nine little wallabies
Ten little wallabies
Hopping all around.*

One little, two little
Three little wallabies
Four little, five little
Six little wallabies
Seven little, eight little
Nine little wallabies
Ten little wallabies
Sleeping in a pouch.*

One mama, two mama
Three mama wallabies
Four mama, five mama
Six mama wallabies
Seven mama, eight mama
Nine mama wallabies
Ten mama wallabies
Jumping up and down.*

One mama, two mama
Three mama wallabies
Four mama, five mama
Six mama wallabies
Seven mama, eight mama
Nine mama wallabies
Ten mama wallabies
Hopping all around.*

One mama, two mama
Three mama wallabies
Four mama, five mama
Six mama wallabies
Seven mama, eight mama
Nine mama wallabies
Ten mama wallabies
With joey in the pouch.*

* It is necessary to add extra notes to the melody for these additional words.

(The wallaby is a small or medium-sized kangaroo in Australia. Some wallabies are as small as a rabbit. A joey is a baby wallaby.)

DINOSAUR MARCH
(Melody: When Johnny Comes Marching Home)

Dinosaurs marching one by one—hurrah, hurrah
Dinosaurs marching one by one—hurrah, hurrah
Dinosaurs marching one by one
They are having so much fun
As they all head for the swamp
Down to the swamp, down to the swamp
Boom, boom, boom!

Dinosaurs stomping two by two—hurrah, hurrah
Dinosaurs stomping two by two—hurrah, hurrah
Dinosaurs stomping two by two
Will they stop to eat and chew?
As they all head for the swamp
Down to the swamp, down to the swamp
Boom, boom, boom!

Dinosaurs growling three by three—hurrah, hurrah
Dinosaurs growling three by three—hurrah, hurrah
Dinosaurs growling three by three
They're looking for some plants to eat
As they all head for the swamp
Down to the swamp, down to the swamp
Boom, boom, boom!

Dinosaurs eating four by four—hurrah, hurrah
Dinosaurs eating four by four—hurrah, hurrah
Dinosaurs eating four by four
They are hungry—they want some more
As they all head for the swamp
Down to the swamp, down to the swamp
Boom, boom, boom!

Dinosaurs sleeping five by five—hurrah, hurrah
Dinosaurs sleeping five by five—hurrah, hurrah
Dinosaurs sleeping five by five
They are so glad to be alive
As they all hide in the swamp
Down in the swamp, down in the swamp
Boom, boom, boom!—Boom!

NUMBER RHYME
(Melody: Skip To My Lou)

One, two—Where's my shoe?
Three, four—On the floor
Five, six—My dog does tricks
Seven, eight—He's so great!
Nine, ten—Sing again! *(shout)*

One, two—The birds coo
Three, four—The lions roar
Five, six—My horse kicks
Seven, eight—I can skate!
Nine, ten—Sing again! *(shout)*

One, two—What do you do?
Three, four—At the shore
Five, six—I do tricks
Seven, eight—That is great!
Nine, ten—Sing again! *(shout)*

One, two—I see you!
Three, four—At the door
Five, six—See the chicks
Seven, eight—At the gate!
Nine, ten—Sing again! *(shout)*

One, two—Here's a few
Three, four—Give me more
Five, six—Potato sticks
Seven, eight—On my plate
Nine, ten—Sing again! *(shout)*

One, two—I love you
Three, four—More and more
Five, six—My heart ticks
Seven, eight—You are great!
Nine, ten—**Time to end!**

COUNT WITH ME
(Melody: first two lines of Twinkle, Twinkle)

Counting, counting, oh what fun!
Will you count with me to ONE?
One. *(spoken)*

I like counting; yes, it's true
Can you count with me to TWO?
One, two. *(spoken)*

Now I ask you, count with me
Please count with me up to THREE.
One, two, three. *(spoken)*

Can you count a little more?
Count with me now up to FOUR.
One, two, three, four. *(spoken)*

Count with me; now don't be shy
We will count as far as FIVE.
One, two, three, four, five. *(spoken)*

Count again; now let's be quick
We will go as far as SIX.
One, two, three, four, five, six! *(spoken)*

COUNT TO TEN
(Melody: Twinkle, Twinkle)

One, two, three, four
Five, six, seven
Eight, nine, ten—now
Once again!

One, two, three, four
Five, six, seven
Eight, nine, ten—now
Once again!

One, two, three, four
Five, six, seven
Eight, nine, ten—now
We can end.

Activities—Numbers/Counting

Visual Aid: Copy, color, cut, and laminate the illustrations found on page 53 and use them on the felt or magnetic board while teaching the children "The Counting Song." Make additional bones, worms, and eggs. Put felt or magnetic tape on the back of each illustration.

Cognitive Skills: Randomly display the illustrations for "The Counting Song." Invite the children to match the correct animal to the correct item associated with the animal. Cut out more pictures of animals and appropriate items for the children to match.

Pre-Math: The children will count with the teacher as he/she points to each animal in the song "How Many Animals?" Make ten copies of the illustrations on pages 54 and 55. (It is not necessary to color the illustrations.) Cut, laminate, and affix felt or magnetic tape on to the back of each animal. Use on the felt or magnetic board. Store each group of animals in a plastic sandwich bag.

Art Activity: Invite the children to make stick puppets for the song "Wallabies." On sturdy paper, make copies of the illustrations on page 56. The children can color the wallabies and cut them out on the rectangle or on the outline of the animal. Secure the mama wallaby onto a large craft stick and the baby onto a small one. Cut an opening in the mama wallaby's pouch and insert the baby stick puppet.

Movement: Teach the class to sing "Dinosaur March" displaying the number of fingers that each verse designates. Demonstrate how to sway your fingers from side to side to the rhythm of the song. Invite the class to repeat this finger action when they march and sing the song.

Class Attention: Select one verse of your choice from the song "Number Rhyme." Ask the children to join in as you repeat it. Sing the selected verse throughout the day in order to get the attention of the children and invite them to join you. Select a different verse each month.

Guessing Game: The children will guess how many items are in a box, container, or pile. Show the children three or four groups of like items such as plastic bears, wooden blocks, wrapped candy, or marbles. Ask them to guess the number of items in a group. Have them join you in counting the items. Vary the amount of items and have the class repeat the guessing game.

HOW MANY ANIMALS?

HOW MANY ANIMALS?

WALLABIES

LITTLE BUTTERFLIES
(Melody: Shoo, Fly)

Fly little butterfly
Fly little butterfly
Fly little butterfly
Fly up high now in the sky.

I saw one butterfly
When I was at the zoo
Another one came by
Now I see there's two.

Fly little butterflies
Fly little butterflies
Fly little butterflies
Fly up high now in the sky.

I saw two butterflies
When I was by the sea
Another one came by
Now I see there's three.

Fly little butterflies
Fly little butterflies
Fly little butterflies
Fly up high now in the sky.

I saw three butterflies
When I walked from the store
Another one came by
Now I see there's four.

Fly little butterflies
Fly little butterflies
Fly little butterflies
Fly up high now in the sky.

I saw four butterflies
When I went for a drive
Another one came by
Now I see there's five.

Fly little butterflies
Fly little butterflies
Fly little butterflies
Fly up high now in the sky.

Trace the butterfly pattern on this page. Cut out five felt butterflies of different colors. Use them on the felt board as you teach this song.

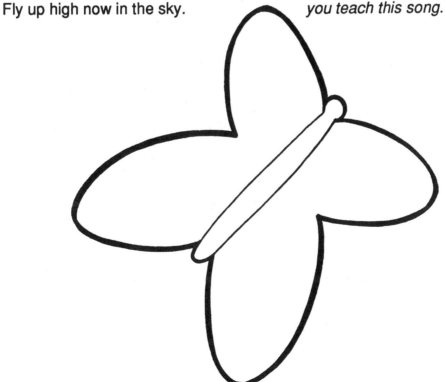

THE FRIENDLY ANTS
(Melody: Ten In The Bed)

There was one little ant
And he called to his friend
"Come with me; come with me"
Well the friend said "yes"
And went with him.

There were two little ants
And they called to their friend
"Come with us; come with us"
Well the friend said "yes"
And went with them.

There were three little ants
And they called to their friend
"Come with us; come with us"
Well the friend said "yes"
And went with them.

There were four little ants
And they called to their friend
"Come with us; come with us"
Well the friend said "yes"
And went with them.

There were five little ants
And they called to their friend
"Come with us; come with us"
Well the friend said "yes"
And went with them.

There were six little ants
And they called to their friend
"Come with us; come with us"
Well the friend said "yes"
And went with them.

There were seven little ants
And they called to their friend
"Come with us; come with us"
Well the friend said "yes"
And went with them.

There were eight little ants
And they called to their friend
"Come with us; come with us"
Well the friend said "yes"
And went with them.

There were nine little ants
And they called to their friend
"Come with us; come with us"
Well the friend said "yes"
And went with them.

There were ten little ants
And they shouted real loud,
"We're here!" *(shout)*

*Ask the children to suggest a few places
that the ants might have been going to,
such as to a picnic, to an anthill, or to a
discarded candy bar.*

FIVE GRIZZLY BEARS
(Melody: Five Little Ducks)

One grizzly bear went far away
To find someone to scare one day
He found a cave and shouted "BOO!"   *(shout "Boo")*
Out came a grizzly—now there are two.

Two grizzly bears went far away
To find someone to scare one day
They found a cave and shouted "EEEE!"   *(shout "EEEE")*
Out came a grizzly—now there are three.

Three grizzly bears went far away
To find someone to scare one day
They found a cave and gave a ROAR   *(roar)*
Out came a grizzly—now there are four.

Four grizzly bears went far away
To find someone to scare one day
They found a cave and shouted "Hi!"   *(shout "Hi")*
Out came a grizzly—now there are five.

Five grizzly bears are going home
You can hear them moan and groan   *(moan)*
"We're so tired" is what they said
Five grizzly bears go back to bed.

MONKEYS AT THE ZOO
(Melody: She'll Be Coming Round The Mountain)

There was one little monkey at the zoo
There was one little monkey at the zoo
He was dancing all around
He was crawling on the ground
There was one little monkey at the zoo.
Here comes another one! *(spoken)*

There were two little monkeys at the zoo
There were two little monkeys at the zoo
They were swinging from the trees
They were picking off their fleas
There were two little monkeys at the zoo.
Here comes another one! *(spoken)*

There were three little monkeys at the zoo
There were three little monkeys at the zoo
They were jumping up and down
They were running all around
There were three little monkeys at the zoo.
Here comes another one! *(spoken)*

There were four little monkeys at the zoo
There were four little monkeys at the zoo
They were scritchin' and a-scratchin'
On their heads, they were a-tappin'
There were four little monkeys at the zoo.
Here comes another one! *(spoken)*

There were five little monkeys at the zoo
There were five little monkeys at the zoo
They were spinning like a top
They would sit right down and stop
There were five little monkeys at the zoo.

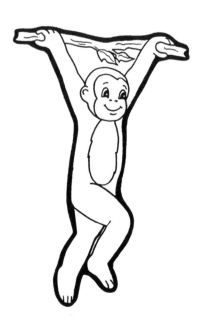

Activities—Numbers/Adding

Movement: The class pretends that they are butterflies as they flutter their wings and fly around the room during the refrain of the song "Little Butterflies." They stop to sing the story verse.

Dramatization: Make character props for the children to wear as they act out the song "Little Butterflies." Copy the large illustrated butterfly found on page 46 onto five colors of cardstock. Punch holes at the top of the paper and tie enough yarn to fit around a child's neck. The class sings the verses and five children are chosen to wear the props and dramatize the song. Select another group of five children to repeat the dramatization.

Social: Play a friendship game. The children sit in a line. One child is selected to choose a classmate while the class sings "The Friendly Ants." The two children hold hands and walk together, in a chain fashion, as the class continues singing the song. The second child picked then selects another child to join them. Continue until all children have been selected and then shout, "We're here!"

Visual Aid: On gray paper, make five copies of the grizzly bear found on page 62. Cut, laminate, and attach felt or magnetic tape to use on the felt or magnetic board with the song "Five Grizzly Bears."

Dramatization: Children can act out the various actions of the monkeys as they sing the song "Monkeys At The Zoo."

Language: Make a booklet with the children. Copy the illustrations of the five monkeys found on pages 63 and 64. Ask the children to select an illustration and discuss what the monkey is doing. Have them dictate a story as you print their words on large tablet paper, inserting the illustration at the appropriate place. Have the children select another illustration and continue with their story until all the illustrations have been chosen.

Cognitive: Play "Who's Missing?" Copy the five monkeys found on pages 63 and 64; display them on a felt or magnetic board. Ask the children to cover their eyes. Remove one monkey from the board. The children are to describe the missing monkey.

FIVE GRIZZLY BEARS

MONKEYS AT THE ZOO

ALICE THE CAMEL
(Melody: Dry Bones)

Alice the camel has five humps
Alice the camel has five humps
Alice the camel has five humps
So go, Alice, go! Boom, boom, boom!

Alice the camel has four humps
Alice the camel has four humps
Alice the camel has four humps
So go, Alice, go! Boom, boom, boom!

Alice the camel has three humps
Alice the camel has three humps
Alice the camel has three humps
So go, Alice, go! Boom, boom, boom!

Alice the camel has two humps
Alice the camel has two humps
Alice the camel has two humps
So go, Alice, go! Boom, boom, boom!

Alice the camel has one hump
Alice the camel has one hump
Alice the camel has one hump
So go, Alice, go! Boom, boom, boom!

Alice the camel has no humps
Alice the camel has no humps
Alice the camel has no humps
Spoken: Does anyone know why Alice doesn't have any humps?
Answer: 'Cause Alice is a horse!

FIVE LITTLE DUCKS
(Melody: Traditional)

Five little ducks went out to play
Over the hill and far away
Father Duck said, "Quack, quack, quack!"
Four little ducks came waddling back.

Four little ducks went out to play
Over the hill and far away
Mother Duck said "Quack, quack, quack!"
Three little ducks came waddling back.

Three little ducks went out to play
Over the hill and far away
Father Duck said, "Quack, quack, quack!"
Two little ducks came waddling back.

Two little ducks went out to play
Over the hill and far away
Mother Duck said "Quack, quack, quack!"
One little duck came waddling back.

One little duck went out to play
Over the hill and far away
Father Duck said, "Quack, quack, quack!"
No little ducks came waddling back.

No little ducks went out to play
Over the hill and far away
Mother and Father said, "Quack, quack, quack!"
Five little ducks came waddling back.

FIVE SUGAR COOKIES
(Melody: Five Green Bottles)

There were five sugar cookies in the cookie jar
Five sugar cookies shaped like a star
Well along came Jimmy, from very, very far
And he ate one cookie from the cookie jar!

There were four sugar cookies in the cookie jar
Four sugar cookies shaped like a star
Well along came Mindy, from very, very far
And she ate one cookie from the cookie jar!

There were three sugar cookies in the cookie jar
Three sugar cookies shaped like a star
Well along came Scott, from very, very far
And he ate one cookie from the cookie jar!

There were two sugar cookies in the cookie jar
Two sugar cookies shaped like a star
Well along came Jasmine, from very, very far
And she ate one cookie from the cookie jar!

There was one sugar cookie in the cookie jar
One sugar cookie shaped like a star
Well along came Brendan, from very, very far
And he ate one cookie from the cookie jar!

There are no sugar cookies in the cookie jar
No sugar cookies shaped like a star
Well along came Grandma from very, very far
And she put more cookies in the cookie jar!

A DINOSAUR STORY

A long time ago, before man walked on the earth, there lived giant lizards called dinosaurs. Some of the dinosaurs liked to eat meat. One of them was Tyrannosaurus, the King of Dinosaurs. He was the meanest of all dinosaurs. Other dinosaurs liked to eat plants. One of them was Anatosaurus, a duckbill dinosaur. Anatosaurus was a very big duckbill dinosaur. He lived during the time of King Tyrannosaurus. Now when King Tyrannosaurus was hungry, he would look for dinosaurs to eat. Some dinosaurs had armor and would fight Tyrannosaurus to protect themselves. Others, like the duckbill dinosaurs, would run to the sea and go into the water. They knew that Tyrannosaurus would not follow them into the water. In the sea, the duckbill dinosaurs could eat the plants that grew in the water and be safe from the Tyrannosaurus.

FIVE DUCKBILL DINOSAURS
(Melody: Sing A Song Of Sixpence)

King Tyrannosaurus looking for some meat
Saw five duckbill dinosaurs—five of them to eat
The king went for the biggest one; he chased him to the sea
The king won't go in water—that duckbill now is free!

Tyrannosaurus went back to look for the other four duckbill dinosaurs.

King Tyrannosaurus looking for some meat
Saw four duckbill dinosaurs—four of them to eat
The king went for the biggest one; he chased him to the sea
The king won't go in water—that duckbill now is free!

Tyrannosaurus went back to look for the other three duckbill dinosaurs.

King Tyrannosaurus looking for some meat
Saw three duckbill dinosaurs—three of them to eat
The king went for the biggest one; he chased him to the sea
The king won't go in water—that duckbill now is free!

Tyrannosaurus went back to look for the other two duckbill dinosaurs.

King Tyrannosaurus looking for some meat
Saw two duckbill dinosaurs—two of them to eat
The king went for the biggest one; he chased him to the sea
The king won't go in water—that duckbill now is free!

Tyrannosaurus went back to look for the last duckbill dinosaur.

King Tyrannosaurus looking for some meat
Saw one duckbill dinosaur—only one to eat
The king went for that lonely one; he chased him to the sea
The king won't go in water—that duckbill now is free!

Activities—Numbers/Subtracting

Visual Aid: On tan paper make six copies of "Alice the Camel" (page 70). Cut out the camels so that you will have: Alice with five humps, four, three, two, one, and no humps respectively. Laminate and secure felt or magnetic tape to each picture. Begin with the camel with five humps; replace it at the end of the verse with the camel having four humps. Continue in this manner until Alice has no humps. Children are delightfully amused with the disappearance of a hump after each verse.

Booklet: Children will enjoy turning the pages of a booklet of "Alice the Camel" while singing the song. Make six copies of "Alice the Camel" on tan paper as described in the above project. Do not cut out the pictures. Laminate and punch holes at the top of each sheet. Secure sheets with steel rings. Make the booklet available to the children with a tape recording of the song.

Dramatization: Invite the children to act out the song "Five Little Ducks." Select seven children to be the five little ducks, the mother duck, and the father duck. Make character props for the children to hold for the dramatization by cutting out simple ducklings out of yellow construction paper and adult ducks out of white paper.

Visual Aid: Cut out five stars from five colors of cardstock to use as star cookies for the song "Five Sugar Cookies." Use markers to simulate sprinkles and candies on top of the cookies; laminate for durability. Substitute the names of the children in your class in place of the names in the song. Have the selected child choose a paper cookie as the class sings.

Snack Time: Bake sugar cookies with the children early in the day so that the cookies will be cool by snack time. Offer the children frosting and candy decorations to spread on their snack time treat.

Create A Scene: Make a scene for the song "Five Duckbill Dinosaurs." Using brown and blue construction paper, divide the area into two sections: land and sea. Copy, cut, and laminate the patterns of the tyrannosaurus and the five duckbill dinosaurs (found on pages 71–73) on to gray paper.

ALICE THE CAMEL

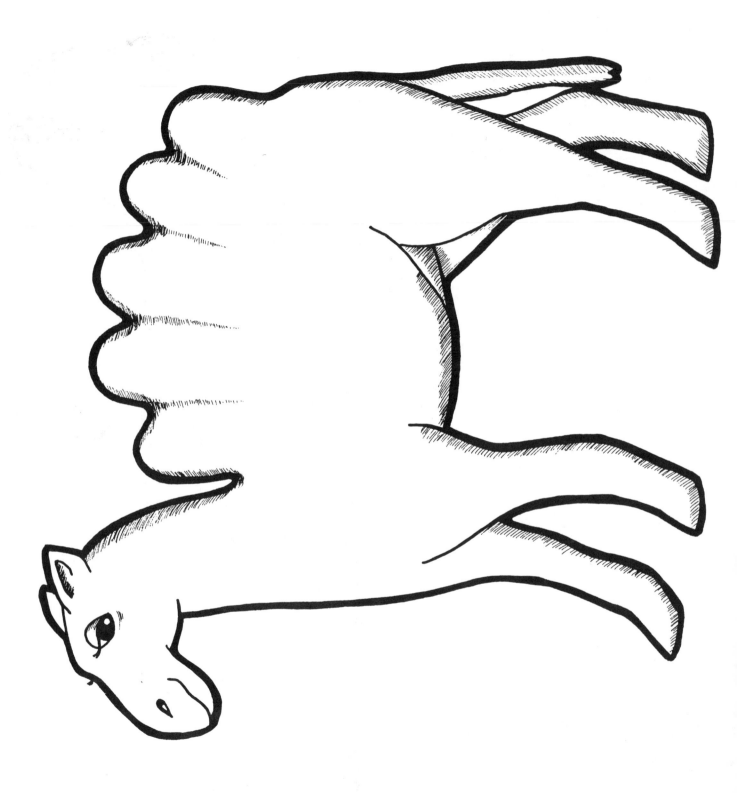

FIVE DUCKBILL DINOSAURS

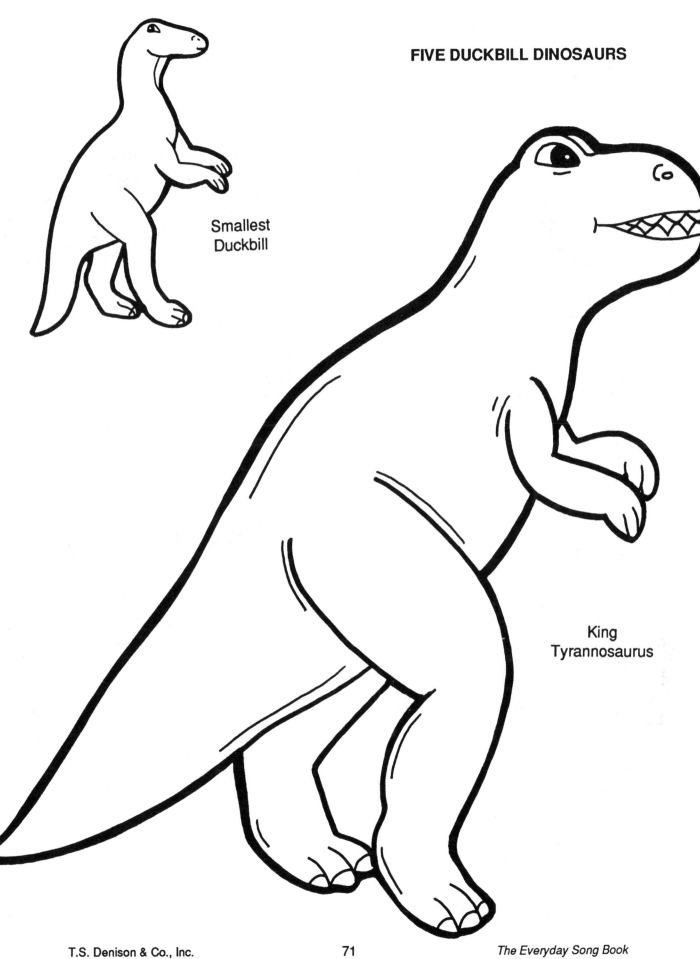

Smallest
Duckbill

King
Tyrannosaurus

FIVE DUCKBILL DINOSAURS

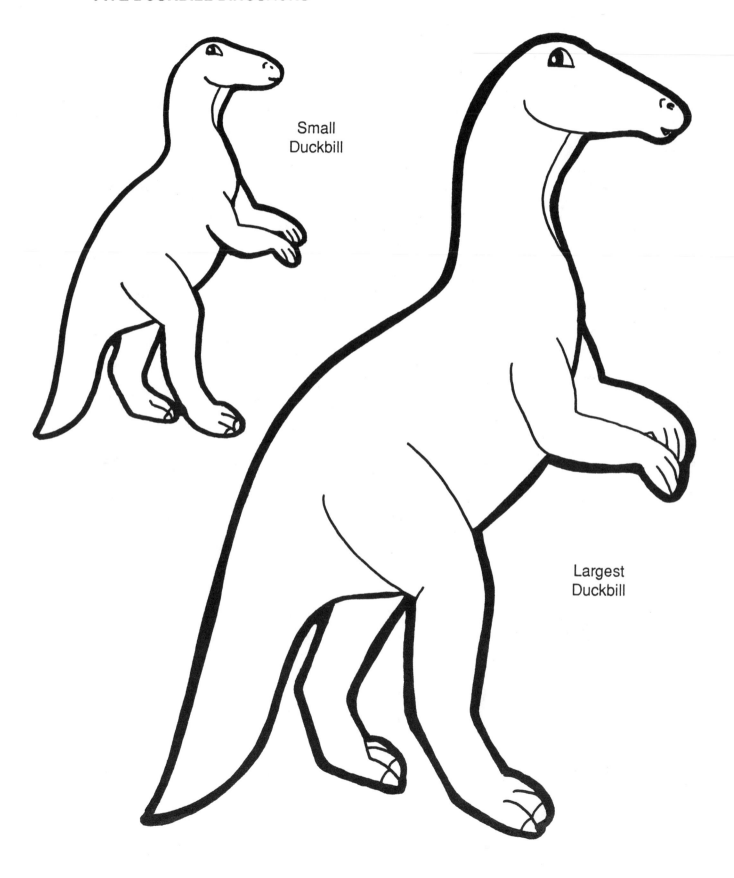

Small
Duckbill

Largest
Duckbill

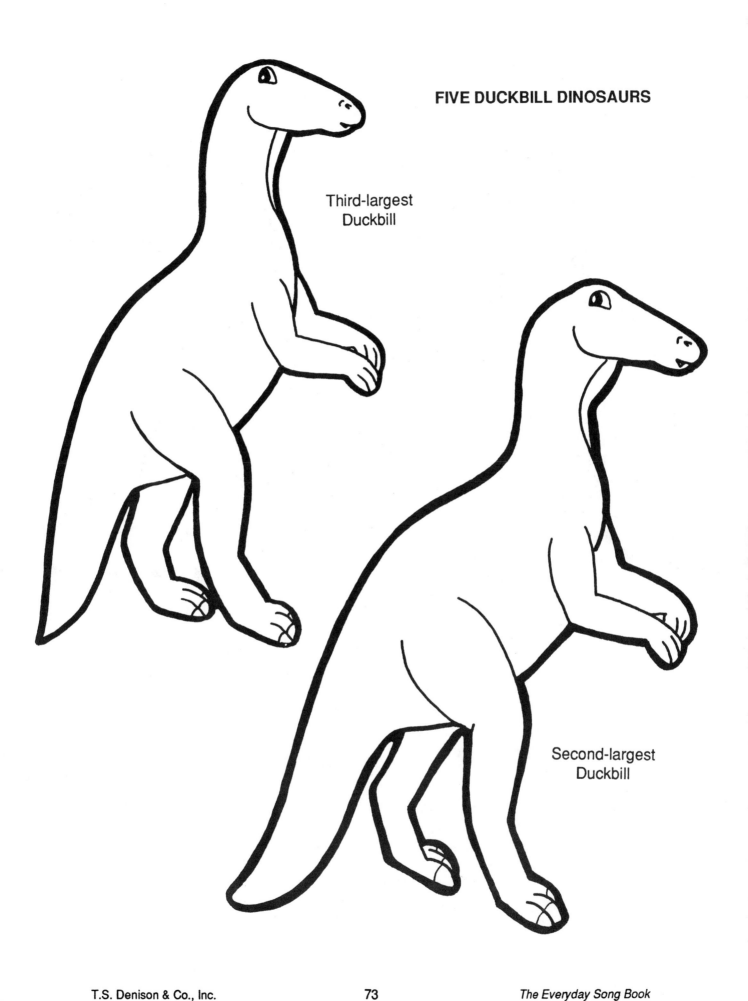

FIVE DUCKBILL DINOSAURS

Third-largest
Duckbill

Second-largest
Duckbill

MEET THE SHAPES
(Melody: first two lines of Twinkle, Twinkle)

Terry Triangle—look at me
Count my sides; there are three
1-2-3 *(spoken)*

Sammy Square—that's my name
I have four sides; they're all the same
1-2-3-4 *(spoken)*

Robbie Rectangle—I have four
Two long, two short but no more
1-2-3-4 *(spoken)*

Cindy Circle—just one line
Make it round; that is fine.

FOUR SHAPES
(Melody: Are You Sleeping?)

Cindy Circle, Cindy Circle
Sammy Square, Sammy Square
Here is Terry Triangle
Here is Robbie Rectangle
They are here!
They are here!

SHAPES
(a chant)

Cindy Circle is my name
One round line gives me fame

Terry Triangle is my name
Just three sides—that's my game!

Sammy Square is my name
My four sides are all the same.

Robbie Rectangle is my name
My four sides are not the same.

MAKE A TRIANGLE
(Melody: Three Blind Mice)

One, two, three; one, two, three   *(point to or draw the appropriate*
Do you see? Do you see?   *line to make a triangle)*
Up the hill and to the top
Down the hill—and then you stop
Straight across; tell me what have you got?
A triangle—a triangle!

MAKE A SQUARE
(Melody: Twinkle, Twinkle)

From the bottom to the top   *(point to or draw the appropriate*
Straight across and then you stop   *line to make a square)*
Straight down to the bottom again
Across and stop where you began
If the lines are the same size
Then a square is your surprise.

MAKE A RECTANGLE
(Melody: Going To Kentucky)

A long line at the bottom   *(point to or draw the appropriate*
A long line at the top   *line to make a rectangle)*
A short line to connect each side
A rectangle you've got!

Now, a short line at the bottom
A short line at the top
A long line to connect each side
A rectangle you've got!

MAKE A CIRCLE
(Melody: Pop Goes The Weasel)

Round and round on the paper I go   *(with finger or pencil, go round*
What fun to go around like so   *and round for a circle)*
What have I made, do you know?
I made a circle!

Activities—Shapes

Visual: Copy, color, cut, and laminate the shape characters found on the pages 77 and 78. Display them on the bulletin board and refer to them for the shape songs and other shape-awareness activities.

Dramatization: Invite the children to personify the four shapes in the chant "Shapes" and the songs "Meet The Shapes" and "Four Shapes." Copy, color, and cut the shape characters found on pages 77 and 78. Glue the characters onto sturdy paper and cut out the background in the appropriate shape. Punch holes at the top of each card shape and tie enough yarn to fit around a child's neck. Select four children to step forth at the appropriate time as the class sings "Meet The Shapes." Select four more children to do the same for the song "Four Shapes" and four others for the chant "Shapes."

Cognitive: Encourage the development of shape awareness. Ask the children to find items in the classroom that contain the shape of a circle, square, rectangle, or triangle. Send a note home to the parents asking them to go around their home with their child looking for the four shapes. Ask each child to bring in four small items representing each of the four shapes.

Social: Play a shape game. Have the children sit in a circle. Pass out paper shapes of different colors and sizes. Call out one of the four shapes. Children holding that shape, no matter what color or size, should stand. As the game progresses, add colors and sizes to your command.

Creative Art: Have the children make a shape collage. Offer them a variety of colors and sizes of squares, rectangles, triangles, and circles. Encourage them to be creative.

Snack: Offer the children nutritious snacks made in the four shapes. Toast, cheese, and jello can be cut into all four shapes. Crackers can be found in all four shapes. Have a "Shape Pot-Luck Week" and invite the children to bring in a snack made in one of the four shapes.

TERRY TRIANGLE

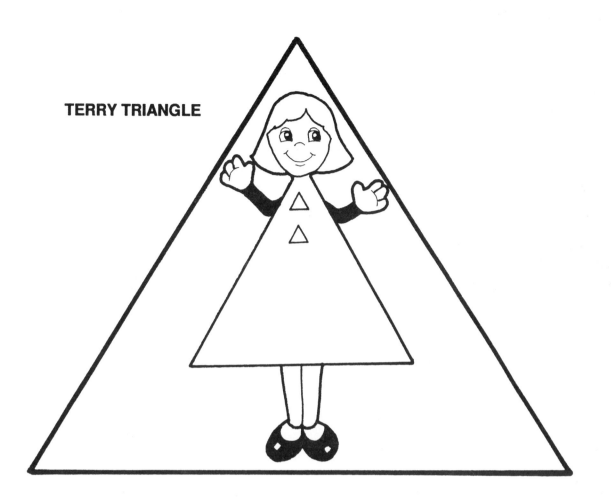

CINDY CIRCLE

ROBBIE RECTANGLE

SAMMY SQUARE

MY BODY
(Melody: Jimmy Crack Corn)

See this head—it is mine
See this hair—it is mine
See this face—it is mine
There's no one else like me.

See these eyes—they are mine
See these cheeks—they are mine
See these lips—they are mine
There's no one else like me.

See this nose—it is mine
See this mouth—it is mine
See this neck—it is mine
There's no one else like me.

See these arms—they are mine
See these hands—they are mine
See these fingers—they are mine
There's no one else like me.

See this chest—it is mine
See this stomach—it is mine
See this back—it is mine
There's no one else like me.

See these legs—they are mine
See these feet—they are mine
See these toes—they are mine
There's no one else like me.

I CAN DO THINGS
(Melody: Skip To My Lou)

Eyes, eyes—I can see
Ears, ears—I can hear
Fingers, fingers—I can touch
Hip, hip, hooray—I'm happy!

Nose, nose—I can smell
Teeth, teeth—I can chew
Tongue, tongue—I can taste
Hip, hip, hooray—I'm happy!

Head, head—I can nod
Hands, hands—I can clap
Feet, feet—I can tap
Hip, hip, hooray—I'm happy!

Legs, legs—I can jump
Arms, arms—I can hug
Lips, lips—I can kiss
Hip, hip, hooray—I'm happy!

FUZZY CATERPILLAR
(Melody: Eency Weency Spider)

Fuzzy caterpillar crawls up my little toe
On my foot and ankle, how far will he go?
To my knee and up my leg—how he tickles me
Then he climbs up on my tummy and soon he falls asleep.

Fuzzy caterpillar crawls up my little hand
Up my arm and shoulder, I wonder where he'll land?
Up my neck and to my ear—how he tickles me
Then he climbs up on my head and soon he falls asleep.

LIL' PETER RABBIT
(Melody: Battle Hymn of the Republic)

Little Peter Rabbit had a fly upon his nose
Little Peter Rabbit had a fly upon his nose
Little Peter Rabbit had a fly upon his nose
He flicked it and it flew away!

Little Peter Rabbit had a fly upon his head
Little Peter Rabbit had a fly upon his head
Little Peter Rabbit had a fly upon his head
He flicked it and it flew away!

Little Peter Rabbit had a fly upon his chest
Little Peter Rabbit had a fly upon his chest
Little Peter Rabbit had a fly upon his chest
He flicked it and it flew away!
Continue the song with other parts of the body.

Variation:
Little Peter Rabbit had a fly upon his nose
Little Peter Rabbit had a fly upon his nose
Little Peter Rabbit had a fly upon his nose
He flicked it and it flew away!

Big Barnaby Bear had a spider on his chest
Big Barnaby Bear had a spider on his chest
Big Barnaby Bear had a spider on his chest
He growled and it jumped right off!

Little Sally Chipmunk had a ladybug on her knee
Little Sally Chipmunk had a ladybug on her knee
Little Sally Chipmunk had a ladybug on her knee
She wiggled and it zoomed away!

Little Freddie Fox had a butterfly on his tail
Little Freddie Fox had a butterfly on his tail
Little Freddie Fox had a butterfly on his tail
He wagged it and it fluttered away!

Little Molly Raccoon had a worm between her toes
Little Molly Raccoon had a worm between her toes
Little Molly Raccoon had a worm between her toes
She touched it and it wiggled away!

Activities—Body Parts

Follow the Leader: Play "Copy Me." Select a child for the class to imitate. The leader must tap different parts of the body. The class then copies the actions of the leader while naming the body part the leader selects.

Listening and Observation Skills: The teacher names a body part for the children to tap and then taps the named body part. The children do likewise. Occasionally, the teacher does not tap the body part that he/she names. The children who realize this shout, "No Way," and do not copy him/her.

Visual: Use the illustrations on page 82 for the song "Lil' Peter Rabbit." Copy the animals and insects on pages 83–86 on to appropriate colored cardstock. Cut out and laminate. Secure felt or magnetic tape on to the back of each picture for use on the felt or magnetic board.

Cumulative Planning: The song "Lil' Peter Rabbit" can be used cumulatively during the school year. Begin with one animal, one insect, and one body part and progress to different body parts. After a few weeks, progress to different animals, and several weeks later progress to a different insect. Use the illustrations of the animals and insects which are found on pages 83–86 on the magnetic or felt board.

Art Activity: Each child will be involved in making a full body self-portrait. Ask the child to lie down on a large sheet of paper. Trace the outline of the child from head to shoe. Add the hair, facial features, a neckline, and a waistband. The child can complete the full-length portrait by coloring the hair, eyes, and clothing.

PETER RABBIT

BARNABY BEAR

SALLY CHIPMUNK

FREDDIE FOX

MOLLY RACCOON

FIVE SENSES
(Melody: Are You Sleeping?)

I have two eyes, I have two eyes
I can see, I can see
With my eyes I see things
With my eyes I see things
I can see, I can see.

I have two ears, I have two ears
I can hear, I can hear
With my ears I hear things
With my ears I hear things
I can hear, I can hear.

I have one tongue, I have one tongue
I can taste, I can taste
With my tongue I taste things
With my tongue I taste things
I can taste, I can taste.

I have one nose, I have one nose
I can smell, I can smell
With my nose I smell things
With my nose I smell things
I can smell, I can smell.

I have two hands, I have two hands
I can touch, I can touch
With my hands I touch things
With my hands I touch things
I can touch, I can touch.

WHAT IS—WHAT'S NOT
(Melody: Are You Sleeping?)

See the ladybug, see the ladybug
She's so small, she's so small
How about the elephant?
How about the elephant?
He is not, he is not.

Hear the thunder, hear the thunder
It is loud, it is loud
How about the snowflakes?
How about the snowflakes?
They are not, they are not.

Taste the honey, taste the honey
It is sweet, it is sweet
How about the lemon?
How about the lemon?
It is not, it is not.

Smell the roses, smell the roses
They smell nice, they smell nice
How about the garbage?
How about the garbage?
It does not, it does not.

Touch the water, touch the water.
It is wet, it is wet
How about the sand?
How about the sand?
It is not, it is not.

MY SENSES
(Melody: I'm A Little Teapot)

Eyes are what we see with; noses smell
The tongue tastes food so very well
Fingers touch and feel while ears can hear
For what we have, let's give a cheer!

I'M SO HAPPY
(Melody: This Old Man)

With my eyes, I can see
I can see most anything
I can see the snails and fishes in the sea
I'm so happy—yes, siree!

With my nose, I can smell
I can smell things very well
I can smell the roses and the minty leaves
I'm so happy—yes, siree!

With my tongue, I can taste
See the smile upon my face
I can taste the honey from the busy bees
I'm so happy—yes, siree!

With my ears, I can hear
I can hear things far and near
I can hear the bluebirds singing in the trees
I'm so happy—yes, siree!

With my fingers, I can feel
I can feel things that are real
I can feel the wool that grows on baby sheep
I'm so happy—yes, siree!

Activities—Senses

Science: Use the activities below to develop sensory awareness.

Hearing: Ask children to identify matching sounds. Collect plastic containers from rolls of film. Fill pairs of containers with identical items such as kidney beans, rice, screws, cotton, and water. Tape the lids onto the containers. Invite the children to shake the containers and find the matching pair.

Smell: Ask each child to identify various scents. Put items of different scents (chocolate, mustard, cinnamon, etc.) in plastic film containers. Pour small amounts of liquids on cotton balls (perfume, peppermint flavoring, vanilla, etc.) and place them in the film containers. Blindfold each child and ask for the name or description of the scent.

Taste: Offer the children a tasting plate of edible items with distinct tastes, such as a lemon (sour), honey (sweet), unsweetened chocolate (bitter), and pretzels (salty). At snack time offer similar items with different tastes such as dill pickles and sweet pickles, and caramel corn and salted popcorn. Discuss the flavor differences.

Sight: Make color paddles for the children to look through. Make the frames from cardboard and tape different colors of plastic cellophane into the frames. Have the children look through the paddles outdoors as well as indoors.

Touch: Make a Feeling Box. Cut a hole on the side of a shoebox just large enough for a child's hand to fit through. Put three or four items in the box for each child to feel and identify.

Directed Activity: Have the children make a booklet of the senses of sight, smell, and touch. Ask them to cut and paste favorite items, pictures, and scenes from various magazines and catalogs onto the pages of the sight category. On the pages designated for the sense of smell, children can squeeze small circles of glue on which they can sprinkle various spices such as cinnamon, garlic powder, ground clove, nutmeg, and rosemary. On the pages classifying touch, the children can glue items such as cotton balls, sandpaper, corrugated paper, silk, and felt.

PEANUT BUTTER-JELLY
(Traditional Camp Song)

Peanut, Peanut Butter—Jelly!*
Peanut, Peanut Butter—Jelly!

First you take the peanuts   *(chant each verse)*
And you pick 'em and you pick 'em   *(pantomime picking peanuts)*
And you pick 'em, pick 'em, pick 'em
Then you smash them and you smash them   *(pantomime smashing peanuts)*
And you smash them, smash them, smash them
Then you spread it on!   *(pantomine spreading on bread)*

Peanut, Peanut Butter—Jelly!
Peanut, Peanut Butter—Jelly!

Then you take the berries
And you pick 'em and you pick 'em   *(pantomime picking berries)*
And you pick 'em, pick 'em, pick 'em
Then you smash them and you smash them   *(pantomime smashing berries)*
And you smash them, smash them, smash them
Then you spread it on!   *(pantomine spreading on bread)*

Peanut, Peanut Butter—Jelly!
Peanut, Peanut Butter—Jelly!

Then you take the sandwich
And you bite it and you bite it   *(pantomime biting sandwich)*
And you bite it, bite it, bite it
Then you chew it and you chew it   *(pantomime chewing sandwich)*
And you chew it, chew it, chew it
Then you gulp it and you gulp it   *(pantomime gulping)*
And you gulp it, gulp it, gulp it.

MmMm, MmMm MmMm—MmMm!   *(hum the melody as if you were singing*
MmMm, MmMm MmMm—MmMm!   *the refrain with your mouth full)*
Peanut, Peanut Butter—Jelly!
Peanut, Peanut Butter—Jelly!

* As you sing "Peanut, Peanut Butter" raise both arms and shake both hands; on the word "Jelly" drop
  arms, bend at waist, and shake hands.

YUMMY PIZZA
(Melody: A Tisket, A Tasket)

A pizza, a pizza
I'll make a yummy pizza
With chocolate chips, and peanuts too
I'll make a pizza just for you!

A pizza, a pizza
I'll make a yummy pizza
With hamburger and hot dogs too
I'll make a pizza just for you!

A pizza, a pizza
I'll make a yummy pizza
With bananas, pears, and apples too
I'll make a pizza just for you!

After singing the song with the children, ask them individually to name two or three items that they would like on their "yummy pizza." If a child responds with only one food item, sing something like this:

A pizza, a pizza
I'll make a yummy pizza
With chocolate chips on the top
I know you'll like it quite a lot!

MY FAVORITE FOOD
(Melody: Reuben And Rachel)

Will you tell us what you're eating?
Tell us what's your favorite food
    (child names food)
Pizza, pizza in the morning
In the night and afternoon!

Will you tell us what you're eating?
Tell us what's your favorite food
    (child names food)
Hot fudge sundae in the morning
In the night and afternoon!

AIKEN DRUM
(Melody: Scottish folk song)

There was a man lived in the moon
In the moon, in the moon
There was a man lived in the moon
And his name was Aiken Drum.

Refrain:
And he played upon a ladle
A ladle, a ladle
And he played upon a ladle
A ladle, a ladle
And his name was Aiken Drum.

And his hair was made out of string beans
String beans, string beans
And his hair was made out of string beans
And his name was Aiken Drum.
(refrain)

And his eyes were made out of cherries
Cherries, cherries
And his eyes were made out of cherries
And his name was Aiken Drum.
(refrain)

And his nose was made out of a carrot
A carrot, a carrot
And his nose was made out of a carrot
And his name was Aiken Drum.
(refrain)

And his mouth was made out of a banana
A banana, a banana
And his mouth was made out of a banana
And his name was Aiken Drum.
(refrain)

Activities—Food Songs

Language Development: "Yummy Pizza," and "My Favorite Food" are songs in which the children can name their favorite foods to change the words of the song.

Puppetry: Give the child a puppet. Ask the child to have the puppet open and close its mouth as if the puppet is eating. Sing the song "My Favorite Food." Direct the question in the song to the puppet. The puppet should respond with a favorite food.

Cooking: Make different kinds of pizza with the children. Cookie dough pizza with fruit toppings and individual biscuit dough pizza with meat or vegetable toppings can be served at snack time. A few "yummy pizza" recipes can be found on page 95.

Visual Aid: Cut a large circle out of a sheet of 12" x 18" yellow construction paper. Draw a face to represent the man on the moon. Laminate. Secure magnetic tape on the back. Color, cut, and laminate the food items on page 94. Secure magnetic tape on the back of each item. Use the illustrations on a magnetic board as you sing the song "Aiken Drum" Provide the children with rhythm sticks or wooden spoons to strike as you sing the refrain "and he played upon a ladle."

Language Development: Invite the children to imagine other foods that might make up the face of the man on the moon, "Aiken Drum." Ask them to close their eyes, touch their hair, and name the food that comes to mind when they feel their hair. What food is round like their eyes? What food do they think of when they touch their nose or smile with their mouth?

Snack Time: Have the children make "Aiken Drum" snacks. Give them cream cheese or peanut butter to spread on rice cakes, round bread, or toast cut into large circles. Provide them with food items such as carrot circles, banana slices, raisins, sliced strawberries, or celery to make the face of Aiken Drum.

Group Activity: Have the children make a wall mural of their favorite foods. Provide them with pictures of food from magazines to cut and paste onto a large sheet of paper to make a collage entitled "Our Favorite Foods."

AIKEN DRUM

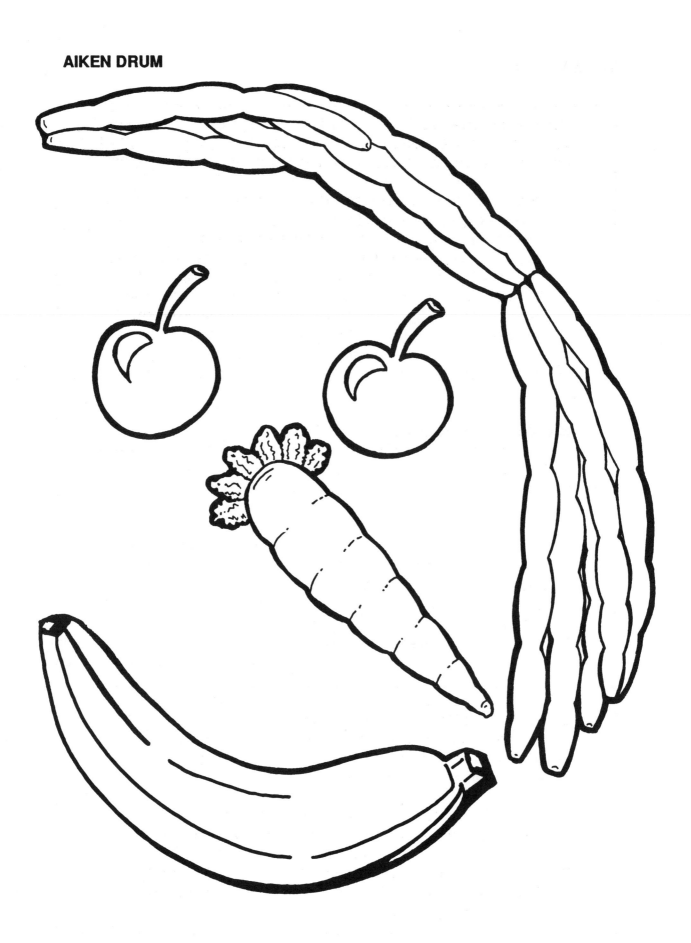

YUMMY PIZZA

Cookie Dough Pizza:
Ingredients: refrigerated sugar cookie dough, 8 oz. cream cheese, 2 tsp. vanilla, 1/3 cup sugar, canned and fresh fruit.

1. Completely cover a well-greased 12" pizza pan with thin slices of cookie dough. Bake at 350 degrees for 8-10 minutes. Cool. (Teacher may choose to prepare the dough at home.)
2. Beat mixture of cream cheese, vanilla, and sugar until softened. Have one group of children spread mixture on cookie dough.
3. Ask the children to bring in canned or fresh fruit such as strawberries, peaches, grapes, mandarin oranges, and crushed pineapple. One group of children can cut the fruit with plastic knives while another group puts the fruit on top of the cream cheese spread.

Biscuit Dough Pizza #1:
Ingredients: refrigerated biscuit dough, pizza sauce, shredded mozzarella cheese, cooked hamburger (crumbled and drained), hot dogs, mushrooms, green pepper, celery, and onions.

1. Separate biscuit dough. Give one biscuit to each child to flatten.
2. Children can help cut up hot dogs and vegetables.
3. Each child spoons sauce and sprinkles cheese on his or her pizza.
4. Each child tops pizza with individual choices of meat and/or vegetables.
5. Bake at 375 degrees. Serve warm.

Biscuit Dough Pizza #2:
Ingredients: refrigerated biscuit dough, shredded cheddar cheese, mushroom soup, sour cream, milk, canned or frozen vegetables: corn, peas, beans, carrots.

1. Separate biscuit dough. Give one biscuit to each child to flatten.
2. Make thick mushroom soup sauce: Children can help mix 1 can of mushroom soup, 2 Tbsp. sour cream, 2 Tbsp. milk.
3. Each child spoons sauce and sprinkles cheese on his or her pizza.
4. Each child tops pizza with individual choices of vegetables.
5. Bake at 375 degrees. Serve warm.

MY PET
(Melody: Mary Had A Little Lamb)

Stephen has a little kitten
Little kitten, little kitten
Stephen has a little kitten
His kitten's name is Tiger.

Kathy has a big white dog
Big white dog, big white dog
Kathy has a big white dog
Her big dog's name is Skippy.

Johnny has a big brown horse
Big brown horse, big brown horse
Johnny has a big brown horse
He likes to ride him fast.

Becky wants a parakeet
Parakeet, parakeet
Becky wants a parakeet
She wants a pretty blue one.

Mark would like a dinosaur
Dinosaur, dinosaur
Mark would like a dinosaur
He would ride him to the school.

ALL THE ANIMALS
(Melody: All The Fish)

All the frogs are jumping up and down
Jumping up and down, jumping up and down
All the frogs are jumping up and down
All day long.

All the birds are flying all around
Flying all around, flying all around
All the birds are flying all around
All day long.

All the rabbits are hopping up and down
Hopping up and down, hopping up and down
All the rabbits are hopping up and down
All day long.

All the horses gallop all around
Gallop all around, gallop all around
All the horses gallop all around
All day long.

All the owls are sleeping in the trees
Sleeping in the trees, sleeping in the trees
All the owls are sleeping in the trees
All day long.

Other verses:
1. All the boys are jumping up and down
2. All the girls are twirling all around
3. All the children sway from side to side
4. All the mommies hug and rock their babies
5. All the daddies hug and rock their babies

DOWN BY THE BAY
(Melody: Traditional)

Down by the bay	*echo**
Where the watermelons grow	*echo*
Back to my home	*echo*
I dare not go	*echo*
For if I do	*echo*
My mother will say	*echo*
Did you ever see a fish	
Washing a dish	
Down by the bay?	

Down by the bay	*echo**
Where the watermelons grow	
Back to my home	
I dare not go	
For if I do	
My mother will say	
Did you ever see a sow	
Milking a cow	
Down by the bay?	

Other verse endings:
Did you ever see a bear
Combing his hair?
Did you ever see a llama
Eating his pajamas?
Did you ever see a snake
Dancing with a rake?
Did you ever see a fly
Wearing a tie?

* Echoes are helpful in learning these songs, but they can be eliminated.

ON GRANDPA'S FARM
(Melody: Down By The Bay)

On Grandpa's farm	*echo**
All the animals play	
They run around	
All night and day	
So come with me	
And you will see	
There are little baby ducks	
And a big mommy duck	
On Grandpa's farm.	

On Grandpa's farm	*echo**
All the animals play	
They run around	
All night and day	
So come with me	
And you will see	
There are little bunny rabbits	
And a big daddy rabbit	
On Grandpa's farm.	

DOWN AT THE ZOO
(Melody: Down By The Bay)

Down at the zoo	*echo**
All the animals play	
They run around	
All night and day	
So come with me	
And you will see	
There are two little bears	
And a big mommy bear	
Down at the zoo.	

Down at the zoo	*echo**
All the animals play	
They run around	
All night and day	
So come with me	
And you will see	
There are two baby lions	
And a big daddy lion	
Down at the zoo.	

Theme: Language

LET'S GO TRAVELING
(Melody: Down On Grandpa's Farm)

(spoken: "Let's go to the deep blue sea")
Oh, we're on our way, we're on our way
On our way to the deep blue sea
We're on our way, we're on our way
On our way to the deep blue sea.

In the deep blue sea, there is a big blue whale
In the deep blue sea, there is a big blue whale
The whale, he swims around like this—Splash, splash!
The whale, he swims around like this—Splash, splash!

(spoken: "Let's go to the wild jungle")
Oh, we're on our way, we're on our way
On our way to the wild jungle
We're on our way, we're on our way
On our way to the wild jungle.

In the wild jungle, there's a hungry lion
In the wild jungle, there's a hungry lion
The lion roars so loud like this—Roar!
The lion roars so loud like this—Roar!

(spoken: "Let's go to the mountain top")
Oh, we're on our way, we're on our way
On our way to the mountain top
We're on our way, we're on our way
On our way to the mountain top.

On the mountain top, there is a mountain goat
On the mountain top, there is a mountain goat
The goat—she makes a sound like this, "Maaa"
The goat—she makes a sound like this, "Maaa"

(spoken: "Let's go to the deep, dark woods)
Oh, we're on our way, we're on our way
On our way to the deep, dark woods
We're on our way, we're on our way
On our way to the deep, dark woods.

In the deep, dark woods, there is a big, black bear
In the deep, dark woods, there is a big, black bear
The bear—he makes a sound like this—Grrr!
The bear—he makes a sound like this—Grrr!

(spoken: "Oh, let's go home!")
Oh, we're on our way, we're on our way
We're on our way back home
We're on our way, we're on our way
We're on our way back home.

Activities—Language

Lyric Writing: Help the children begin writing their own lyrics for the song "My Pet." Ask the children if they have a pet; ask them to tell something about the pet or the pet's name. If a child does not have a pet, ask him/her to name a pet that he/she would like to have, either real or imaginary, as the song indicates.

Movement: Invite the class to imitate the actions of the animals that they sing about in the song "All The Animals." Encourage them to name other animals that they can imitate such as fish swimming in the water and snakes sliding on the ground.

Visual Aid: Photocopy the illustrations for the song "Down By The Bay" onto colored cardstock. Select the most dominant color for the paper and color a few details with markers: light green paper for the watermelon patch and a deep pink marker to color the inside of the cut watermelon. Laminate, cut, and affix felt or magnetic tape to the illustrations. Use on the felt or magnetic board when singing the song with the class.

Creativity: Be creative with any song that the class enjoys. The song "Down By The Bay" is a favorite of many children. "On Grandpa's Farm" and "Down At The Zoo" are simple verses sung to the melody of "Down By The Bay." These songs can be used on field trips to the farm and to the zoo. Add more verses with the children. Create other songs for different excursions.

Create-A-Scene: Copy, color, and cut the illustrations for "Let's Go Traveling" found on pages 105 and 106. Paste the illustrations on colored construction paper: light green for the jungle, dark green for the woods, blue for the sea, and brown for the mountains. Place a picture of an airplane in the center of your four scenes and dramatize an adventurous journey with the children as you sing the verses of "Let's Go Traveling."

bear combing
his hair

snake dancing
with a rake

llama eating
pajamas

sow milking
a cow

watermelon
patch

fish washing
a dish

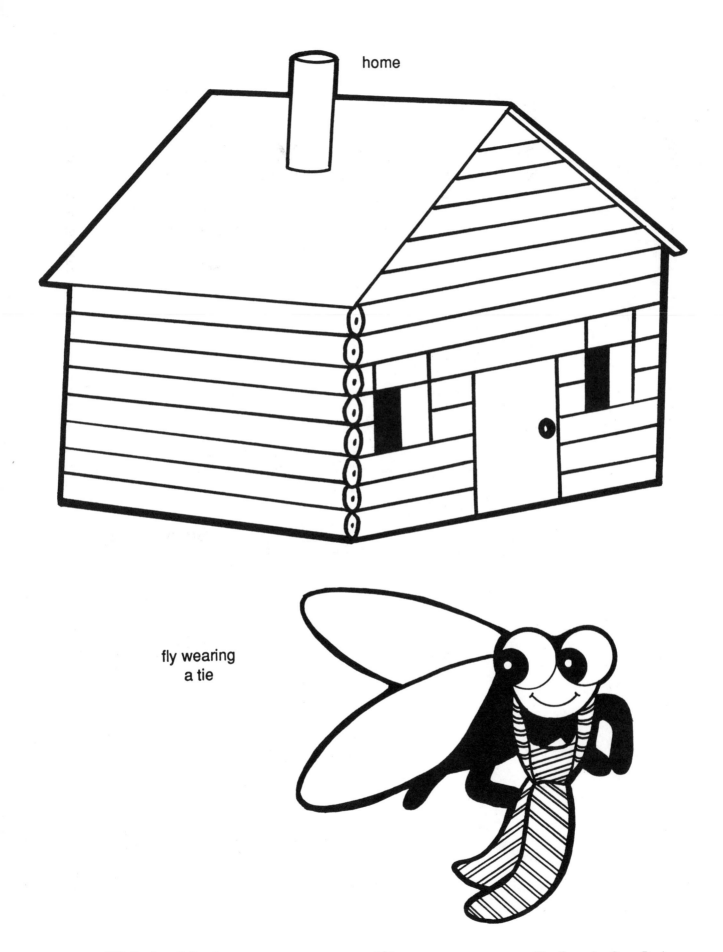

home

fly wearing
a tie

Billy Boy

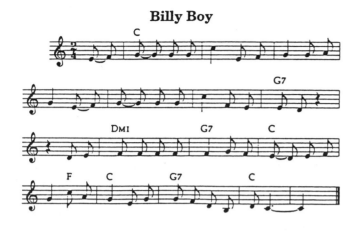

Chiapenecas

Bingo

Did You Ever See A Lassie?

Blue Bird

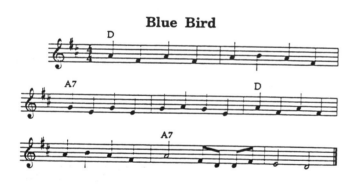

Do Lord

Boom, Boom, Ain't It Great To Be Crazy

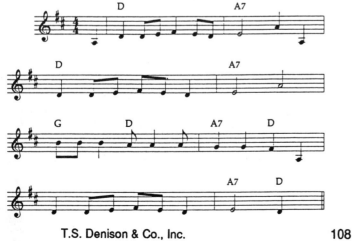

Down By The Bay

Dry Bones

Down By The Station

Eency Weency Spider

Down On Grandpa's Farm

The Farmer In The Dell

Five Little Ducks

Mary Had A Little Lamb

My Bonnie Lies Over The Ocean

Mary Wore A Red Dress

Michael, Row The Boat Ashore

Oh, A Hunting We Will Go

The Muffin Man

Oh, Susanna

The Mulberry Bush

She'll Be Comin' Round The Mountain

Shoo, Fly

Sing A Song Of Sixpence

Skip To My Lou

Ten In The Bed

Ten Little Indians

This Old Man

Three Blind Mice

A Tisket, A Tasket

When Johnny Comes Marching Home

Twinkle, Twinkle, Little Star

You Are My Sunshine